REBECCA TUCKER

A MATTER
OF TASTE

A FARMERS' MARKET DEVOTEE'S SEMI-RELUCTANT ARGUMENT FOR INVITING SCIENTIFIC INNOVATION TO THE DINNER TABLE

COACH HOUSE BOOKS, TORONTO

first edition

Published with the generous assistance of the Canada Council for the Arts and the Ontario Arts Council. Coach House Books also gratefully acknowledges the support of the Government of Canada through the Canada Book Fund and the Government of Ontario through the Ontario Book Publishing Tax Credit.

LIBRARY AND ARCHIVES CANADA CATALOGUING IN PUBLICATION

Tucker, Rebecca, 1986-, author
    A matter of taste : a farmers' market devotee's semi-reluctant argument for inviting scientific innovation to the dinner table / Rebecca Tucker.

(Exploded views)
Issued in print and electronic formats.
ISBN 978-1-55245-367-4 (softcover).

    1. Food supply. 2. Food industry and trade--Moral and ethical aspects. 3. Food industry and trade--Economic aspects. 4. Sustainable agriculture--Moral and ethical aspects. 5. Sustainable agriculture--Economic aspects. 6. Agricultural innovations.
I. Title. II. Series: Exploded views

HD9000.5.T83 2018   363.8   C2018-904953-7
                                                  C2018-904954-5

A Matter of Taste is available as an ebook: ISBN 978 1 77056 555 5 (EPUB), ISBN 978 1 77056 556 2 (PDF).

Purchase of the print version of this book entitles you to a free digital copy. To claim your ebook of this title, please email sales@chbooks.com with proof of purchase. (Coach House Books reserves the right to terminate the free download offer at any time.)

Dedicated to my nonna, Enrica, through whom
all food had power.

For the uninitiated, or anyone who doesn't self-identify as a 'nineties kid,' I guess, Dunkaroos were small, individual-portion-size plastic bins of cookies, adjoined to even smaller plastic bins of cake frosting. The crunchy former were meant to be dipped into the creamy latter. It was an absolute masterstroke of snack-food concepting: sugar on sugar, with a customizable delivery mechanism. When I was in grade school, these were *the* It Snack. But they never once entered my lunch box.

My mother ran the house, as far as food was concerned (as far as a lot of other things were concerned, too). And she had (and has) a strict sense of what constituted food fit for her family to eat. This discriminating sense of good food vs. bad food, born partly of her upbringing in an Italian immigrant household where even peanut butter was foreign and processed, and partly of a typically parental sort of common-sense, five-a-day-style healthy-eating ethos. Broadly, this meant that packaged foods – junk foods, in other words – were verboten. Specifically, this meant no Dunkaroos.

But I lusted for them. I lusted, too, for Vachon snack cakes filled with oily, cloud-white cream; for chocolate-covered granola bars studded with chocolate chips instead of nuts and seeds; for *actual* chocolate bars, scaled down to kid size and packed alongside Lunchables (for which I also lusted, despite not having any idea of what bologna tasted like); for snack-sized bags of potato chips, for cans of soda – for all the things the other kids got to eat for lunch, but from whose consumption I was prohibited by a mother who didn't think children (or anyone) should eat processed foods.

So I stole them.

I wanted what I could not have so badly that I snuck into my classroom during recess and raided my classmates' backpacks. Over time, I was so emboldened by my successful string of thefts that I started pilfering candy from my teacher's desk. I'd eat it on the way home, or in my bedroom, after dark. Eventually, overcome by guilt – and having been almost caught in the act – I fessed up to my parents, my teacher, and the principal. It was kind of traumatic, and it was all because of junk food.

This didn't change anything in our pantry at home. As far as everyone – myself included – was concerned, I was a deviant and a transgressor, tempted by sugar and MSG; what I wanted was Bad Food, and *I* was bad to want it.

This conflagration of actions of moral good (and moral bad) and one's eating habits is not a revelatory idea, not even when applied to the petty lunchtime crimes of a ten-year-old girl. Our eating habits have long been defined in part by a sense of morality, of separating the *good* food from the *bad* food. We are meant to feel a certain way (virtuous, clean, pious) when we eat 'good' food, and the inverse (out of control, irresponsible, ugly) when we eat – or simply desire – food that is 'bad.'

But what constitutes food on either side of the moral divide has been a moving target. For my mother, and her mother, good food meant food whose ingredients they recognized – nothing processed, nothing boxed. Over time, that understanding would have evolved to include a few twentieth-century conveniences, like store-bought crackers, supermarket eggs, and cured meat from a deli counter instead of a neighbour's basement. But despite these few concessions to modernity, my childhood eating habits were remarkably, unusually (and, if you were to ask me, infuriatingly) clean and, well, *good*.

In 2018, however, those twentieth-century conveniences – the boxed crackers, deli meats, and probably-not-free-range eggs – don't quite pass muster. In response to the industrialization of our food systems, food that is recognized as *good* is no longer simply food that is healthful; the moral needle has moved toward food that is organic, food that is local, food that supports a farmer whose name you know, and, perhaps above all else, food that has been affected by as little human intervention as possible.

Stretched to its logical conclusion, this new food moralizing should mean we're all buying food that saves the planet. But stretched to its *practical* conclusion, this has simply meant that feel-good foodie-ism has become more of an aesthetic than a powerful political movement.

Despite years of proselytizing from luminaries like Mark Bittman and Michael Pollan, farm-to-table cooking and farmers' market shopping remain rarefied practices, possible on a recurring (never mind constant) basis to those with not only the surplus money it takes to buy into these supposedly sustainable systems, but the surplus time to spend learning why they ought to. Farms and markets, despite their salt-of-the-earth origins, have become the arenas of the elite. And as the global population skyrockets while the average household income for younger generations continues to stagnate, it is increasingly impractical to imagine that food-system salvation will be delivered in a Williams-Sonoma farmers' market tote. The belief in one's moral goodness should have nothing to do with how much locally grown kale is in one's diet. And besides, the unflappable attachment to farmers' markets and organic produce can be damaging in its own right; obstinate partisanism, in food as in politics, doesn't seem to be moving the needle much these days.

I am confident in the belief that our broken food systems are fixable. And I'm not alone. At the University of Guelph's Arrell Food Institute, for instance, Evan Fraser, the Canada Research Chair in Global Food Security, is leading a think tank called Feeding 9 Billion, aimed at developing food systems that will feed the planet's population once it hits its projected nine billion people in the year 2050. Fraser, one of Canada's – and, indeed, the world's – most prominent voices on food security and the future of sustainable food, believes that vertical farming, artificial intelligence, and data-based farming are key to the future of food. In Florida, Kevin Folta, a horticultural sciences professor, is advocating for the adoption of crop-saving genetic technology. Kimbal Musk (yes, Elon's brother) has started an 'accelerator' for urban farming. John Deere is adopting smart farming machinery that uses GPS technology and machine learning to eliminate waste and create efficiencies. In New York, a company called Agritecture has cornered the market on urban-farming consulting, tapping into the controlled-environment architecture industry – essentially, indoor farming – that will be valued at an estimated $9 billion in the next two years.

In this book, I look at four important aspects of the future of food, all of them underpinned by the urgent need to reevaluate when and how to – and if we should at all – apply morality to our food buying, growing, and producing choices. First, whether or not the farmers' market ethos is truly sustainable, considering both the cost of producing these goods and the cost of purchasing them. Second, how the urbanization of the human race has ignored the need to integrate agriculture into city planning (and how this can be remedied). Next, how innovation and lab science can help conventional *and* organic farmers produce hardier, more efficient crops and more reliable yields. And finally, how information technology and computer science is offering truly outside-the-box, future-thinking solutions to current food crises.

Dig in!

A great meal is an experience that nourishes more than
your body.

— Ruth Reichl, *Delicious!*

You'll never know how good something can be until you
change your act and maybe risk it, and if you're wondering
how good a cracker can be, you'll never know until you try
a Triscuit.

— 1970s jingle for Triscuits

For as long as there has been commercial interest in the
mass production of food, there have been efforts to
make it seem as wholesome as the stuff that grows on
farms (or the stuff that eats the stuff that grows on farms).
And to make consumers feel that opting for the newer,
faster, more convenient approach to dinner (which might
come from a can, a freezer bag, or a takeout window) was
not only a safe idea, but a good one – 'good' as in nutritious,
as well as in virtuous.

One advertising cliché used to suggest this equivalency
involves transposing processed items with the whole foods
they might replace on your dinner table. Early advertise-
ments for Kraft Dinner, that all-Canadian pantry staple,
sold the boxed mac and cheese as Kraft 'home cooked'
dinners. A McDonald's print ad from 1969, meanwhile, ran
beneath the text 'Jimmy's mother knows McDonald's
hamburgers are 100% beef' – the food was wholesome, in
other words, because it was approved by that stalwart

bastion of domesticity: the matriarch. The TV series *Mad Men* played off this, too, in its fictionalized 1969 ad campaign for the chain Burger Chef: in her pitch, Peggy Olson uses the proximity of the household television to dinner tables to illustrate how modern families are starving – 'and not just for dinner,' she says, but for attention. The campaign tag, 'Family supper at Burger Chef,' says precious little about the food itself, but uses the convention of the family dinner table as a way to say, in not so many words, 'This is just like dinner at home – if not better.'

Of course, this is all marketing magic – Kraft Dinner, McDonald's, and, presumably, the fictional Burger Chef are as processed as processed can be (just look at the colour of the, ahem, 'cheese' involved). Falling for the idea that tucking into a box of Kraft Dinner – especially now that the formula has been rejigged to include no artificial colouring – or serving one to your family is a forgivable offence, if food-based decisions do in fact require forgiving, makes sense, given the prominent tag lines and slogans that claim it's wholesome for you, for your family, and for the planet.

In fact, similar marketing messaging goes into KD's virtuous-seeming counterpart. Having purchased both (for research, and for hunger!), I know that Annie's Home-grown macaroni and cheese – an organic boxed pasta option – is a little different from Kraft Dinner in taste (less salty) and caloric value (about a third lower). But the way both products are sold is not altogether different: Annie's uses a cute bunny as the mascot for its entire product line, suggesting nostalgia, childhood, and, again, wholesomeness; a 2017 Kraft ad titled 'Family Greatly' has parents discussing how challenging it is to find time to be a perfect parent (luckily, KD takes only about ten minutes to make). Where these two paths diverge in the woods is most evident when you dig into each company's mission statement: for Kraft, it's 'helping people around the world eat and live better.' For Annie Homegrown: bringing organic food to, ahem, 'everybunny.'

On the surface, this seems like an instance of apples and, well, fancier apples. But the difference between 'better' food and 'organic' food is significant. For one thing, 'better' – which we'll take here to mean healthy, or health*ier* – is subjective, and open to debate: one person's healthy might be another person's sodium-rich. But organic is a set-in-stone concept, enforced at a federal level in the United States and Canada, and defended fiercely by its disciples as the best option for you, your family, and your planet. You can evangelize for Annie's, because you can evangelize for organics. And many do. It's much more difficult to evangelize for 'better food,' even though that's what we all really want, because that term isn't as concrete. Annie's has the advantage of being on a clearly defined side.

But Kraft has the advantage of price. A box of KD sets you back $1.47 at Walmart, and Annie's Homegrown Organic Macaroni & Cheese costs about a dollar more. So it's not entirely clear whether, in this example – and many others – organic is the better option for everyone, every time. Not everybunny can stretch their grocery budget, but everybody deserves better food.

The reason for KD's low cost is, of course, not exactly a pretty picture – it's a mass-produced product, one made relatively cheaply from relatively cheap ingredients. But the reason for its continued, entrenched existence – and the continued, entrenched existence of packaged meals like it – has a bit more nuance. In his 2004 book *In Praise of Slow*,

Canadian journalist Carl Honoré charts the treacherous rise of processed. Referencing the meal-in-a-pill from the fictionalized future of *The Jetsons*, Honoré says, 'Even growing up in a foodie household, I remember liking the idea of an all-in-one meal pill. I imagined gulping it down and heading back outside to play with my friends.' Indeed, the real-life convenience-food revolution that was happening in the early 1960s, when *The Jetsons* was on the air, was born of a newfangled need for speed and convenience; as North American families were engaged in rapid urbanization, and as more North American women entered the workforce to keep up with a burgeoning consumer culture, cooking three square meals from scratch was becoming an untenable luxury.

The value – both personal and economical – of fast-and-ready, however, precedes the TV dinner by a few decades, at least in the West. 'Hurry,' Honoré writes, 'took its place at the dinner table during the Industrial Revolution. In the nineteenth century, long before the invention of the drive-thru burger bar, one observer summed up the American way of eating as "gobble, gulp and go."' (Indeed, judging from the information I've gleaned from my Italian family, this was uniquely American: traditionally, my Mediterranean ancestors wouldn't walk down the street with so much as a cup of coffee, much less a full meal.) 'As our forebears moved into cities and lost touch with the land,' Honoré continues, 'they fell in love with the idea of fast food for a fast age. The more processed, the more convenient, the better.'

Hence a heady period of processed foods invading sit-down restaurants and at-home kitchens, with Campbell's soup pridefully listed on diner menus, and TV dinners replacing Sunday roasts (which, Honoré points out, enraged men who believed their wives were growing lazy). The ads changed, too: Kraft Dinner, for instance, became 'How to eat well, in spite of it all,' touting the boxed meal's ease of preparation; McDonald's emphasized low prices and convenience over wholesomeness.

The reliance – particularly in North America – on fast, cheap foods resulted in a snowballing growth of the industries in which those foods are produced. And with that growth came certain sacrifices. The industrial pace of packaged-food production changed the way we eat, but also the way we farm. And the capitalist motivation for the development of these foods may have meant minimal concern for environmental sustainability or nutritional density.

These changes, if you consult the champions of sustainability, mean we have fast/junk/packaged/processed foods to blame for any number of social and literal ills. We're fat because of sugar and dumb because of fat; we've ruined the planet with the commodity crops we grow to make Twinkies and feed McDonald's-destined cows; we don't know our families because we spend more time in front of the computer, wolfing down space food, than at the dinner table, where surely we'd bond with each other in the candlelit fantasy of some better time.

Not that there's a shortage of data on how our current food practices are damaging both our bodies and our planet. An estimated 26 per cent of earth's farmable land is used to grow livestock feed that will be given to pigs and cows that will be transformed into highly processed products; the sheer amount of packaging involved with processed foods has had and will continue to have an astronomical environmental impact; and the cost – both literal and to our planet – of transporting packaged goods from processing plant to grocery-store shelves is significant. And, in truth, we do all seem to be in pretty rough shape.

So it's tempting to blame processed food – a tidy little scapegoat with, from a sustainability POV, few redeeming factors. Plus, it's kind of evil: the people who make it have designed this type of food to tap into our desires. They make it, and they make us want it bad enough to buy it over and over again.

In his 2015 book *The Dorito Effect: The Surprising New Truth about Food and Flavor*, Canadian food writer Mark Schatzker – who defines junk food as 'food that tastes like something that it is not' – explains how food scientists have engineered packaged, processed foods to have such big, bold, obnoxious flavours that we have come to distrust big, bold flavours when we encounter them in nature: we have forgotten that food can taste remarkable on its own, because we are so used to food tasting remarkable through additions, subtractions, and adjustments.

Plus, junk food has been finely engineered to appeal to some of our most base instincts and evolutionary cues: we often feel pleasure when we eat, which is our brains associating specific flavours with specific nutritional compounds. We feel good, in other words, because we're getting what we need: we like the sweetness of a tomato because it means ripeness, which means a denser nutritional composition. But when we eat junk food we can find ourselves tricked into thinking we're getting what we need, nutritionally; junk food makes us feel good, and our brains think we're feeling good because we're eating good food. When, in fact, we're just eating a bag of ketchup chips that our brain receives as a chemical pleasure similar to that offered by a very ripe tomato. When I interviewed Schatzker in 2015, he pointed something else out: our brains' correlation of flavour to nutrition might actually prevent us from overeating, when we're eating real foods. When we eat three ripe peaches, we inherently know that we've gotten the nutrients we need, and we stop eating; that cue doesn't exist with the fruit's tangy, artificial counterpart, Fuzzy Peaches, because the nutrition doesn't exist either – even though the flavour does.

Schatzker is an interesting player in the food-sphere of the early twenty-first century. He's something of a moderate, as comfortable around a snack as he is enthusiastic about a science-grown tomato; more of a reporter than an evangelist for any one type of eating (though, admittedly, he does lean measurably away from packaged stuff, even if he's not banging on doors to warn us of its evils). In other words, he's not all that much like Michael Pollan.

In 2006, Michael Pollan released the defining tome of the foodie era that, in many ways, sought to put to rest the idea that processed food in any measure is a viable option for humanity. *The Omnivore's Dilemma: A Natural History of Four Meals*, which quickly became a bestseller and earned Pollan a James Beard Foundation Book Award, sought to answer one (deceptively, beguilingly, grabbingly) simple question: 'What should we have for dinner?'

Pollan's book at once defined and catapulted into the zeitgeist the food-borne anxieties that would come to define the next decade for food activists and concerned diners. In it, the American journalist puts everything from factory farming to foraging to fast food under the microscope, with the stated goal of determining the best food to eat. His conclusion, practically, is that the Perfect Meal, as he calls it, is one that is partly foraged, partly hunted, and allows him 'to eat in full consciousness.' Which is to say that, almost immediately, Pollan gives up the idea that the 'best' food means, purely, the healthiest food – the food that is best for us to eat, for the sanctity of our bodies. The best food, to him, is the food that allows for a pretty significant helping of righteousness.

In the book's foreword, Pollan notes that the question of what to eat, for humans, has historically been almost strictly utilitarian: evolutionarily, the omnivore's dilemma – that is, the human's dilemma – centred, first, on determining which of a plethora of available foods would not kill us, and second, on deciding which of these foods could serve as good sources of the nutrients, vitamins, and minerals we require to stay alive. A lot of the time, we figure this out by tasting things, and subconsciously associating biological responses with flavours: the collagen in bone broth might have once helped your body recover from a bad cold, for instance, which explains why you might crave chicken soup the next time you have a flu. (In *The Dorito Effect*, Schatzker calls this 'biological wisdom,' though he also explains that we're not as instinctively wise to the evolutionary benefits of flavour as we used to be, on account of our prolonged exposure to the artificial stuff).

Pollan addresses some of this, too. 'Many anthropologists believe that the reason we evolved such big and intricate brains was precisely to help us deal with the omnivore's dilemma...' he writes. 'Omnivory offers the pleasures of variety... But the surfeit of choice brings with it a lot of stress and leads to a kind of Manichean view of food, a division of nature into The Good Things to Eat, and The

Bad.' Pollan was joined in 2007 in the pursuit of revolutionizing dinnertime by Canadian writers Alisa Smith and J. B. MacKinnon, whose *The 100-Mile Diet: A Year of Local Eating* brought to the fore the virtuous idea of 'locavorism'; Barbara Kingsolver's *Animal, Vegetable, Miracle: A Year of Food Life* followed shortly thereafter and doubled down on the assertion that the best food is the stuff that comes from your own backyard. Pollan returned in 2008 with *In Defense of Food: An Eater's Manifesto*, and firebrand *New York Times* columnist Mark Bittman released *Food Matters: A Guide to Conscious Eating* the same year.

In 2009, the moral quandary of what's good to eat, and what's not, hit the big screen with *Food, Inc.*, a documentary co-produced by Eric Schlosser (who, eight years earlier, eviscerated McDonald's and Co. with his book *Fast Food Nation*). The film, based on *The Omnivore's Dilemma* and narrated by Pollan, was called 'literally gut-wrenching' by NPR and 'one of the year's most important films' by the *San Francisco Chronicle*. *Food, Inc.* was nominated for an Academy Award. It lost out to dolphin doc *The Cove*, but that didn't matter: the film succeeded in putting onscreen – thereby making it far more widely accessible and discussed than it was in print – Pollan's message that eating right doesn't just mean eating nutritiously – it means eating morally. (Not coincidentally, NPR's review labelled Pollan and Schlosser 'embodiments of conscience.')

Food Inc. firmly cemented a shift in the North American consciousness, popularizing the idea of 'sustainable food systems' by focusing on exactly the opposite (one of the largest criticisms lobbed toward the film is that it doesn't offer up much in the way of solutions). Up to that point, prevailing grocery-aisle concerns were largely personal:

'What harm does food cause me when I eat it?' Because Pollan et al. turned the lens outward, identifying systemic issues plaguing the industrial production and distribution of food in the twenty-first century, the concerns became political, ideological, and moral: 'What harm am I doing when I eat food?'

You can see what happened here: the food industry has been completely and utterly polarized. The use of the words *good* and *bad* are not without impact; the result is that every type of food falls into one camp, with little if any flexibility. But when things become brittle, they break.

In 2011, the fast-food giant Chipotle released an animated advertisement that laid out, in no uncertain terms, how we ought to feel about bad food. The spot – soundtracked by a plaintive Willie Nelson cover of the Coldplay song 'The Scientist' – begins with a farmer in his field, tending to a herd of eight pigs. The farm then grows to include cows, then more cows, then more pigs. Soon, there is infrastructure to match: pigs are shipped along factory assembly lines, pumped full of pills, fattened beyond recognition, and pressed into cubes, before being packed into freight trucks. The ad returns to the farmer back in his field, now at nightfall, plagued with guilt: dark storm clouds, filled with imagery of pills, industrial waste being pumped into waterways, and pigs behind bars surround his hanging head. He snaps out of it, the sun comes up, and he dismantles his farm's buildings, allowing his pigs and cows to once again roam free. The land turns over, from industrialized to pastoral, and the farmer loads a single wooden crate into a…Chipotle delivery truck, as the words 'CULTIVATE A BETTER WORLD' glide onto the screen. The two-minute spot was named the world's best TV campaign at Cannes in 2012.

The messaging in the spot was clear. It wasn't so much 'Eat Chipotle' as it was 'Feel like shit for eating anything that isn't as ethical as Chipotle': before the starring farmer turns back the clock on his farm, he is literally weighed down by the moral heft of his capitalist decisions. His world literally goes from dark to light when he eliminates 'science and progress' (sorry, Chris Martin) from his work. The spot was heavy-handed and effective, sure, but at the end of the day it is no longer entirely honest: after a devastating E. coli outbreak in 2016, the chain cut ties with local farmers by as much as 83 per cent, citing safety concerns, effectively eviscerating the core tenet of the chain's 'Food with Integrity' mission and putting it in the same leagues as the McDonald'ses from which it had sought to ideologically separate itself.

In *Jamie's Ministry of Food*, celebrity chef Jamie Oliver fumed over a family who preferred takeout over cooking: 'They've got a plasma screen, a Sky box, mobile phones and Nike trainers, but they'll sit on the floor and eat out of Styrofoam boxes seven days a week. There's a new kind of poverty, and it's fucking knowledge poverty,' as if families ought to feel shame for spending their money on anything but farm-fresh food (and his cookbooks, I suppose, for knowledge). My colleagues are regularly apologetic for eating packaged food. In Michael Pollan's Netflix series *Cooked*, the writer extolls homemade bread as essential to life as he kneads and bakes in his well-appointed New York kitchen. My friends and I swap food-science stats like baseball cards, sharing the latest research on GM this and industrial that, hoping to keep up with all the moral shortcomings of so-called 'bad' food, in order that it might prevent us from ever so much as remembering how good it tastes.

But Hershey chocolate is delicious. Mobile phones are essential. Packaged food saves valuable time (and baking bread takes up too much of it). Sometimes industrial food is the only option. And, with apologies to Willie Nelson, Chipotle is still a goddamn fast-food chain.

Most food shoppers are, by this point, familiar with the terminology associated with 'good' food, because we see it everywhere food is sold, or we're aware of it subconsciously, at the absolute least, as words that exist. The most potent, loaded, and ubiquitous of these is, of course, *organic*: literally, this means food grown in the soil, without pesticides or synthetic fertilizers; ideologically, the term has over time evolved into a catch-all for food that is small-w whole, appearing on store shelves unmodified, unprocessed, unpackaged – barely touched by human hands.

Thinking more about our food is smart economically, politically, socially, and environmentally. The issue with today's sustainable-food conversation is that it often has little to do with the actual *thinking* part. Instead, we're often working in shorthand, creating an alienating, elitist system of beliefs that accompanies the eating of organic foods – or, if not organic, then whole foods, clean foods, or simply good foods – that goes well beyond the things we actually, y'know, eat. Rather than leading to improve our global food systems, empower the hungry, or guide policy, many conversations about sustainable food are often just further rehashing of the same three actions: attempting to convert junk-food-loving sinners through guilt, recruiting the wealthy to special-interest and expensive diets, and generally preaching to the choir – who are themselves blindly faithful.

For many, the zealotry with which food is approached – and discussed, evangelized about, and proselytized on –

mirrors religious fanaticism. It's not enough to have a grocery list; these days, that list is often guided by a 'food philosophy' that might run the gamut anywhere from vegetarianism to organic-only to purchasing nothing that comes in a bag or box. (Michael Pollan's 'Eat food, not too much, mostly plants' is certainly a food philosophy.) The way we eat can be used as a marker of our individual values and principles the same way religious affiliation might – you can tell a lot about a person by whether or not she knows the difference between free run and free range. And just like religious devotion, which is meant to encourage thinking outside of oneself but is too often reduced by the devout to empty piousness and self-righteousness, so too are most food philosophies inward-facing and outward-guilting. It's easy to *say* that buying organic crackers is divine; buying into that idea, for a lack of concrete evidence, is, for most, little more than an act of faith.

I grew up in Guelph, a small city in southern Ontario as renowned for its agricultural college as for its staunch environmentalism. As a kid, I didn't know much about food outside of the fact that I liked it, and I liked to eat a lot of it. But had I been aware of the sorts of food politics that Pollan et al. were in the process of writing about, an inventory of my childhood home might have put my mind at ease.

My mother did groceries twice a month, on Saturday mornings, and on those days the fridge would be filled with fresh fruit and vegetables (mostly seasonal), cheese, milk, and eggs. There were some packaged goods as well – Kraft peanut butter, Wonder Bread (always whole wheat), hot dogs, dry pasta. We had a chest freezer in the basement that was crammed with bricks of homemade stock, sauce, and stew, plus blanched vegetables from our expansive outdoor garden and baked goods from Nonna, who lived nearby. I can count on one hand the occasions I remember eating a meal at home that wasn't made mostly from scratch. My mother, who moved to Canada from Italy in the 1950s, grew up in a house where peanut butter was a foreign substance and stewed tripe was regularly on the menu because it was cheap (and, if you ask her, delicious). We ate uncommonly well at home, by most accounts, because my mother was the one doing the shopping and the cooking; she didn't know how to feed us any other way.

Pollan and his contemporaries might have taken another view of my mother's grocery habits. That Wonder Bread? Pollan wouldn't even call it bread. Kraft peanut butter? Full of chemicals and produced by one of the world's largest, maybe most evil, food conglomerates. Hot dogs? Tubular manifestations of unnatural industrial-farming practices – completely, utterly objectionable. But my mother, who bought only diet soda and never once sent me to school with a packet of Dunkaroos, thought she was doing everything right.

In 2009, after both my sister and I had flown the coop, my parents had a lot more time to themselves. By then, I had been living in Toronto for four years, and had taken an active interest in food, both preparing it and exploring what the city had to offer. I was beginning to learn about the difference between organic and conventional produce, the importance of buying free-run eggs, the impact of shopping at the farmers' market – and I started sharing this information with my mother. I also saw *Food, Inc.* It didn't seem particularly novel to me, since an upbringing largely absent of packaged, processed, and fast foods – thanks to my mother – had given me the impression, by default, that these were things to be avoided.

My mother saw *Food, Inc.*, too. She had begun filling the time she would have otherwise occupied with my sister and me by learning more about food. She read *The Omnivore's Dilemma* and started paying closer attention to the provenance of her groceries. But the real sea change took place when my mom bought *Eating Animals*, Jonathan Safran Foer's 2009 polemic against factory farming. It was the last straw – my mother decided that the most moral path forward was to quit eating animals altogether.

I found this frustrating – by that point I had independently determined that the best way to encourage sustainable agricultural practices was to vote with my dollar, and so I was spending a lot of my student-loan money on grass-fed beef and happy chickens. But my mother suddenly felt she had been making poor decisions all along. She began to worry about how much damage she'd done – not just to her family but to the planet at large. It was a double-edged sword: she felt she was complicit in everything she'd been reading about, and it was time to stop; and she had always understood good food to be integral to a good life, but if she'd been feeding us bad food all along, what might that imply about her abilities as a parent?

This is a huge success on the part of the sustainable-food people, insofar as their key messaging to non-believers – that there is a profound moral wrong in continuing to choose Bad Food – hits home and inspires change. The thing is: my mother had the luxury of making that decision. By then she had time, to read and research but also to shop and cook. And there was pre-existing interest in food and its related politics, which led to her doing research in the first place – without that core interest, that desire to be good and do better, it wouldn't have mattered how much free time she had or how many good-food proselytizers crossed her path. Contra Pollan, Oliver, and their ilk, it takes more to correct bad food behaviours than the desire to do penance for a chance at salvation. That works well in the church, where prayer can be performed in lieu of monetary donation to the virtuous cause, but not quite so well when money is the only option.

And to move away from the more religious allusions, there is also an element to modern sustainable-food consumption that veers into the exclusive-clubbish, if not the overtly cultish. Farmers' markets, once literally a place for actual farmers to sell their actual farmed goods, have their own aesthetic – often borrowed by wedding planners – and are scenes upon which a certain kind of shopper can build social capital as much as a place to pick up a pint of green beans. To be clear, I'm not entirely immune: my Insta-gram feed is as full of food pics and #markethauls as the next food-loving Instagrammer's. Social media is a great way to tell people who you are and what you stand for; photos of markets are a great way to let people know you're part of the sustainable-food club.

The sustainable-food club has a very specific set of rules for entry, one of which is a goodly amount of disposable income. The decision, as the *New York Times*'s virtuous-eating proselytizer Mark Bittman characterizes it, to choose good food over bad is a luxury, because what is largely defined as bad food – processed food, mass-produced food – is cheaper than the good stuff. The problem isn't that farmers' markets and small producers have been identified as alternatives to industrial food production, it's that they've been labelled the *only* alternative. (Surely there is middle ground between Burger King and eleven-dollar artisanal sourdough?) As long as there is only good and bad, but no room for good-ish, bad-ish, and the occasional transgression that won't get you kicked out of the sustainability club altogether, just a small fraction of people will be permitted to participate in the only system that those in the know say will save us all – and if the club is so small, how much of a difference is it actually making? And for whom?

'If everybody could just remember how bad they felt after eating bad food, they would stop doing it,' Mark Bittman said last fall, to a room full of Torontonians gathered in support of Community Food Centres Canada. Sitting in the audience, I began deconstructing this sentence as soon as it was out of the revered cookbook author and food journalist's mouth – in fact, I put so much mental energy into taking it apart that I barely heard anything else he said all night.

'How bad they feel' as in how physically bad? Or 'how bad they feel' as in how emotionally bad, which is to say, how guilty? Does the 'bad food' to which he referred mean junk food? And what tier of junk food – fast food from a restaurant, or packaged food from the supermarket? Or is 'bad food' something more esoteric: food that is immoral, that comprises junk food but extends from industrial meat and factory-farmed tomatoes to farmers' market produce that's grown on a small scale but not certified organic?

Do I forget how bad – emotionally, physically, morally – I feel when I eat junk food? Or when I eat food whose provenance I am not 100 per cent certain of? Do I actually feel bad in the first place? And is eating bad food – any type of bad food, no matter how you define *bad* – always such a conscious decision?

For Bittman, I knew from reading his books and articles over the years, bad food is junk food. At his talk in Toronto he consistently alluded to how deplorable he finds it that children have access to vending machines in grade schools, especially ones that sell anything other than, I don't know, baby carrots and corn on the cob. Bittman advocates for avoiding food that your grandmother wouldn't recognize – 'junk food' might be packaged or 'processed food': stuff with hard-to-pronounce ingredients, seemingly unnatural additives, that comes in strange colours and unusual shapes, all of which seems to suggest we ought not to put it in our bodies in the first place. Or, at least, that our forebears wouldn't – or, more accurately, didn't, because it didn't exist.

This isn't new to Bittman's script. He has, since the early aughts (and before – which is to say, before it was cool), advocated for a more mindful, conscientious approach to shopping for, cooking, and eating food. To be clear, I admire the effort, and have found myself on occasion shopping and cooking with his suggestions and precepts in mind. But his advocacy – and the same-minded advocacy of others like him – has given way to a sort of foodie evangelism. You know the one: it champions a return to the small farms, farmers' markets, and artisanal production methods of yore as a panacea for the issues plaguing our global food systems. And this approach has, indeed, become more than a mere trend. Nostalgic food practices are now broadly accepted as the path forward, so much so that the conversation surrounding what constitutes good, or sustainable, food is entirely divisive: on the one side, we have those who prefer the small-business, small-farm, nose-to-tail, sometimes-organic approach; on the other, we have, well, convenience and mass commerce. And in the middle – in the place that would serve the most people and have the greatest impact – there appears to be almost nothing, owing to the stalemate of the other two polarized sides.

During the Q&A, one audience member challenged Bittman on this line of thinking: how, she asked, could he justify suggesting everyone eat heirloom tomatoes, when so few people can actually afford whole foods to begin with, never mind the heirloom stuff?

He cut her off: 'I never said that. I never said heirloom.'

'You say, "Don't eat anything your grandmother wouldn't recognize,"' she countered, to which Bittman said yes, and she would recognize a supermarket tomato. It was the only time during the entire event that he showed his teeth, and also the only time that his messaging was challenged.

I'm not going to put words in Mark Bittman's mouth. He might not have meant heirloom, but he definitely didn't mean vacuum-packed. Bittman, Honoré, and to a lesser extent Schatzker (if only because he will admit to a weakness for the occasional processed snack) are firmly in the anti-processed-food camp, the one that suggests taking time with your food rather than taking your food to go. The idea is good, but the execution is exclusive – and excludes the very important variable of time. Even if you can afford the heirloom veg, the utopian idea of cooking and sitting down to eat three meals a day is a distant fantasy – what's the use in suggesting that it's the most valuable way forward when we've firmly established ourselves in the gig economy, where we're driving ride shares on top of our nine-to-fives and renting our apartments to strangers on weekends? Slow food is a nice idea, but its only enemy is not fast food. These days, the whole stupid world is fast; if Norman Rockwell were around, he'd be painting half the nuclear family FaceTiming the other half from the back of an Uber.

And anyway, how do we, in 2018, define processed? Adherents to 'clean eating' might be (or almost certainly are) more inclined toward a rigid, restrictive definition of the term, when it comes to food, that includes nothing that hasn't hit the table soon after it was picked, harvested, caught, or killed. That would, of course, exclude things like canned vegetables, cured meats, and fermented beverages: as soon as you use a verb as an adjective before an ingredient, it becomes processed food. How much are we meant to cut out?

I mean, what about the Triscuit?

I can't remember the first time I ate a Triscuit cracker, but it definitely happened at home. And I know I used to eat them a lot: I worked after-school jobs in high school and, having a huge appetite, would melt cheddar cheese over a plate of Triscuits in the microwave almost nightly between 9:30 and 10:00 p.m. (this is, by the way, a snack I still enjoy frequently and recommend highly; Triscuits are that rare cracker that holds its structural integrity under heat).

It was odd to have Triscuits at home, because, as a rule, we didn't keep packaged, processed foods around. But my mother bought them because, to her mind, the processing was extremely minimal – they only have three listed ingredients: whole wheat, oil, and salt.

The history of Triscuits involves some very particular celebrations of innovation and processing – though the cracker itself has maintained a Bittman-friendly three ingredients throughout its more than one-hundred-year lifespan. In 1901, the inventor and businessman Henry D. Perky relocated his company, Natural Food, from Massachusetts to Niagara Falls, to capitalize on the hydroelectric power generated by the Falls. Natural Food was, at the time, known for two products: Shredded Wheat and Triscuits, both of which used a manufacturing process designed by the machinist William Ford (if you think about it, Triscuits and Shredded Wheat are structurally similar – Ford's machine is to thank). Perky's early Shredded Wheat packaging, as a result, boasted that the product was a 'Wonder of the Age'; Triscuit boxes featured an image of the cracker superimposed over an illustration of Niagara Falls, with lightning bolts shooting out in all directions – 'BAKED WITH ELECTRICITY,' the box declared. There's something about the assertion 'with electricity' that, in the 1920s, would have implied that the Triscuit was somehow futuristic and, for that reason, appealing.

Or, to put it differently: it was human intervention – processing – that made the Triscuit. The addition of electricity meant that the food was processed – all three or three hundred ingredients of it – and the explicit highlighting of that processing meant that, at that point at least, the process was a plus.

That was then, but now each box of Triscuits assures shoppers and snackers that the crackers are 'GMO-free.' This is a tale as old as marketing itself: you have to take the temperature of your audience to know how to sell to them. In the early half of the twentieth century, it might have been a terrific idea to market foods as futuristic, but the more we've learned about the evils of industrialized, well, everything, the more we've wanted industry out of our food. And in the context of food, moving away from industrialization and back toward whole, slow, local foods is more than the desire of a demographic – it's a grassroots movement. As Naomi Klein says in her seminal book *No Logo*, 'throw a few liberal platitudes their way and, presto, you're not just a product but an ally in the struggle.' So: Triscuits are non-GMO, Starbucks is fair trade, McDonald's is striving toward carbon neutrality. We don't have to forget that food is processed; we just have to know that it is somehow otherwise good. Even if, as in the case of the examples above, that is not necessarily the case.

This perhaps adds a moral strike against processed food: in marketing to the cause, they're deceiving the consumer into thinking they're changing eating habits. 'We, the eaters, have power,' writes *Washington Post* columnist Tamar Haspel. 'Enough people say "clean labels!" –' by which she means labels suggesting that a packaged food fits the tenets of clean eating '– and we get clean labels. It's an idea that undermines the narrative that we are victims of a food supply foisted upon us. Collectively, we can change things. Ultimately, we will get the food supply we demand. Too bad we are squandering that power by demanding clean labels.'

The general consensus, when it comes to the ethical argument against processed food, is that processed means packaged, packaged means fast, and fast means lazy. And laziness is morally reprehensible – sloth is, after all, one of the seven deadly sins (thanks, Catholic school upbringing). This dichotomy simply doesn't allow for a modern way of living, where work, family, commuting, and then perhaps work on top of work take up the time we might otherwise invest in preparing our meals from scratch. There is much to bemoan about the corporations that process food: they have played a large part in the environmental degradation of our planet, for one thing, and continue to do so through industrial-scale farming, processing, and packaging operations. Fast-food restaurants don't pay service workers a livable wage, although some of them are among the most lucrative companies in the world. Industrial farms often employ migrant labourers, paying them well below what citizenship-holding individuals would demand. Monopolies like Monsanto have compromised swaths of land and bullied farmers out of work. There are – and will continue to be – many reasons to mistrust the intersection of capitalist interest and food production. But to pretend the solution is that we all simply transition back to our grandparents' eating habits is to ignore a century's worth of socio-economic evolution and to eliminate the possibility for any accessible middle ground in how we view – and will continue to grow, market, and sell – food going forward.

In *The Omnivore's Dilemma*, Pollan reflected on a North America in which nutritionists guided what types of foods we put in our grocery carts. But today, the prevailing concern surrounding food isn't what it could do for us; rather, it is what it has already done (and what has already been done to it) by the time it hits our plates. The definition of 'The Good Things to Eat, and the Bad' has shifted since Pollan first considered it – and in a direction very much driven by his book and others like it. What Pollan and his contemporaries discuss is, largely, how unsustainable our industrial food complex is on a large scale. And it's true that *The Omnivore's Dilemma* – as the book's tenth-anniversary edition claims on its back jacket – has transformed the way thousands of people think about 'the politics, perils and pleasures of eating.' It has done so by bringing the concept of 'ethics' to the dinner table.

As any first-year philosophy undergrad can attest, the application of ethics to any series of thoughts, actions, and decisions is a hugely subjective exercise, with hundreds of competing theories. Largely, the understood definition of 'ethical eating' follows consequentialist-utilitarian principles: the actions largely understood to be 'good,' as they relate to food, are the actions that will, in theory, produce the most significant positive benefit to the greatest number of people.

Much of the time, this definition excludes the personal. (It's not without irony that there is a branch of hedonist ethics – the branch that believes the most ethical action is the one that produces the most pleasure – called *epicureanism*.) But more than not affording much wiggle room for personal gratification, which is often a by-product of ethical eating rather than a stated goal, the twenty-first-century tenets of ethical food consumption disregard the reality that not everyone who wants to – and knows how to – eat ethically is able to do so.

Whole foods free of industrial or scientific intervention are – despite over a decade of farm-to-table advocates insisting that growing demand for sustainable supply will tip the scales of affordability – still exponentially more expensive than the alternative. And for those whose thinking about food has been transformed without the capital to act upon it, Pollan's actionable lessons become less fuel for revolution and more fodder for guilt and shame.

This is because knowing what food is 'good' – and what type of eating is 'ethical' – naturally leads to an understanding of the obverse. If good food is moral food, bad food is not just food that's unhealthy, but also food that we ought to feel ashamed to eat. Shouldn't we be doing better simply because, with all those ethical-eating bestsellers out there, we know better? In *A Bone to Pick*, Mark Bittman seems to think so: his columns positing long-term solutions to systemic issues within the current food system have simplistic titles such as 'Make Food Choices Simple: Cook' and aphorisms like 'Healthful food is delicious food, traditional food, real food.' If it were so easy to act upon the advice such books offer, we'd be well on our way to undoing decades of systemic damage to our food systems.

Ethical eating is more than a great through line for a bestseller – it has become a marketing buzzword. These days, the most prevalent terms in food marketing are words whose implication is not practical but moral. And one specific word comes up a lot: Cheerios' 'Good Goes Around' campaign centred on a jingle that contained the lyrics 'Start with the good, and the good will come back to you,' and 'The circle of good makes the world better, too.' Starbucks's 'Good Feels Good' ad, which asks individuals 'What does good feel like?' – answers range from 'helping others' to 'love,' 'compassion,' and 'joy.' The fast-food chain A&W, which relaunched and rebranded in 2015, wrapped its stores in the sort of bright-green window dressing that implies green grass, much of it emblazoned with a meaningless slogan: 'Good food makes good food.' This is beyond marketing nostalgia – this is marketing righteousness.

These are not necessarily brands whose practices would get the *Food, Inc.* seal of approval – and they are certainly foods whose products are processed, and therefore fit well within the boundaries of what might be classified as 'bad.'

Nevertheless, they have capitalized on the ubiquitous belief that eating well means buying food that is somehow metaphysically good, and that this practice will result in the world becoming a better place.

Moralizing about food is not new. But the framing, in the West, of food as ethically Good or ethically Bad is a uniquely twenty-first-century invention (Eastern philosophies and religions have long-established codes of conduct and morality focused on food: witness Buddhist vegetarians and so forth). Previously, the lion's share of moralizing done around food involved vice and virtue, where cakes and pastries were 'guilty pleasures' to be avoided by dieters (largely women). The casting of cheap, prefab fast food as unvirtuous, however, is a slightly newer convention. As *Guardian* columnist Kathryn Hughes wrote in 2014, responding to a University of Toronto study that found that exposure to fast food can make urban-dwellers impatient: 'The panic around the moral and psychological damage of fast food – forget the obesity debate – is a familiar one… [Fast food represents] ignorance, indifference, a wilful inability to imagine a better way of feeding the future.'

In other words, added to the shame of being unable to buy into the farmers' market economy is now the oppressive layer of guilt that if you can't afford to eat whole, ethically, Good food, you're not just ruining your health – you're also ruining the whole planet, now and forever.

Brent Preston is a journalist-turned-farmer who runs the New Farm, a farm and sometimes event space in Ontario. Preston's farm is 'deliberately low-tech in terms of our production systems, because we think it's more sustainable: providing more employment, being more environmentally sustainable. The way I put it sometimes is that industrial agriculture is interested in chemicals, and we're interested in biology.' He works closely with a number of programs and organizations involved in food insecurity, such as Community Food Centres Canada, and agrees with the idea that good food is not accessible to all people – though, being an *organic* farmer first, he looks at this from a very specific point of view: 'I think that people who talk about organic food being not accessible from a price standpoint, we're talking about a very specific portion of the popula-tion,' he says. 'People who can't afford organic are people who are having trouble affording to buy food, period. People focusing on buying local food is great, it's great to buy local, but we sometimes use that to set a low bar for ourselves. There's destructive agricultural practices happening every-where, including locally.'

Preston believes that more government money should be earmarked for organic farming operations, to bring costs down for the consumer. It's a nice idea, and a fair one – farmers at large don't get a huge share of the subsidy pie – but it seems like a manufactured problem (organic food is the only truly good food) looking for a solution that already exists in allowing for a compromise: that the consumption of whole foods over fast foods is a net win, organic or not.

My food-buying habits underwent a fundamental shift in 2009. I graduated from university, meaning I no longer had access to my student line of credit; rather, I had to start paying it back. I had recently moved to a neighbour-hood far away from the independent grocery store that had previously been a five-minute walk from my apartment door; I didn't know where to get organic, fair-trade products (not that I could afford them, anyway). I started working a full-time job that required me to commute two and a half hours a day; any time I had to build wholesome meals from scratch was replaced with exhaustion, fatigue, and anxiety. My apartment had no outdoor space in which to grow vegetables, not that I had any time for gardening. I had all the knowledge, education, and awareness to make ethical food decisions, but none of the resources. I bought cheap produce and cheaper pre-made meals. I felt constant shame. But there was nothing I could do.

Michael Pollan is here with me – kind of. 'Farmers who get the message that consumers care only about price will themselves care only about yield,' he writes. 'This is how a cheap-food economy enforces itself.'

But by focusing on the supply side of a 'cheap-food economy,' Polan erroneously implies that the demand side is calling the shots. He essentially suggests that consumers who care only, or most, about price have *chosen* to care only, or most, about price, by remaining purposefully igno-rant of the big-picture, moral implications of their eating habits – rehashing the age-old assumption that the poor are stupid and lazy – and thereby electing to simply not make the most ethical possible decision. In reality, low-income shoppers are often highly motivated to make 'good,' educated decisions about food and eating, but lack the resources to fully do so. And with the ubiquity of main-stream messaging about ethical eating, this creates a great weight on the conscience.

It is largely, widely accepted that processed food is often cheap because it is subsidized – though this itself might be a half-truth (and an awfully convenient one at that, depend-ing on which side of the ethics debate you happen to find yourself). *Washington Post* columnist Tamar Haspel, a consistent voice in the ongoing conversation surrounding food policy in the United States, suggested in a December 2017 column that we've gotten the math wrong here: subsidies exist, yes, and where food is concerned they disproportionately favour companies and conglomerates that produce packaged and fast foods (and are largely absent when it comes to supporting farmers), but they aren't a wholly suitable scapegoat: 'Yes, junky food ingredients get much more subsidy money than fruits and vegetables,' she wrote in her column. 'And I've argued against a system that has taxpayers subsidizing foods that are worse for us, rather than those that are more nutritious. But here's the key overlooked fact: Produce is inherently much more expensive to grow than the grains that are used in fast- and processed-food production, and that difference dwarfs the difference in subsidy levels.'

This happens a lot: identifying an enemy that we're all already a little bit wary of (in this case, large multinationals with government ties), assuming that that enemy must be the enemy in all cases, and accepting facts that demonstrate this without seeking alternative information. Of course, confirmation bias exists in the fight for good food, but so much confirmation bias seems to have shielded advocates from the idea that there are two (or three, or four, or infinite) sides to the slow-food story – as a result, many have been railing against one thing and advocating for its opposite, without considering that the best approach might be attacking the issue from all sides. Which, in this case, would mean considering how to mitigate the cost for farmers of growing produce, while at the same time attempting to funnel subsidy cash away from junk food. To borrow some terminology from slow-food advocates: a large problem deserves a holistic problem-solving strategy and, in the case of food, that strategy might be more mechanized than holistic. But we'll get there.

Very little progress has been made in pitting Good and Bad foods against one another in the well-meaning attempt to correct systemic failures in our global food systems. I wonder whether the whole thing ought to be considered on a sliding scale, rather than as a question of moral absolutes. Otherwise, we'll find ourselves continually mired in a sustainability stalemate.

2

Fresh Cities

Do I dare to eat a peach?
> – T. S. Eliot, 'The Love Song of J. Alfred Prufrock'

For me, mid-August has always meant two things: tomatoes and peaches.

Tomatoes were a staple in my mother's kitchen, but for two weeks a year we were overrun with them. Between my aunt, my mother, and my nonna, all of whom had enormous vegetable gardens in their respective backyards – and, since they're Italian, dedicated plenty of space in each plot to tomatoes – it was a race against time to pick, eat, cook, and can as many of the fleshy red fruits as we could each day. On visits home, after I moved away, they'd pawn as many tomatoes off on me as possible (to little protest from my end).

The peaches were (and are) a different story. No one we knew grew peaches, so we weren't dependent on our own little network of backyard gardens to announce their glorious growing season. But my nonna, who was born and raised on a farm, had a second-nature sense of knowing when to expect the prime time for fruits and veg, even if they were only available to us at the grocery store. We never ate peaches in the winter, because, as the matriarchal wisdom had taught us, it just didn't make sense. But for two (sometimes three) weeks in August, they were on hand every day.

Perhaps because of how uniquely seasonal peaches were in my home growing up – and for how short a time – I have a particular affection for them. Seasonality was a consideration my mother made when she bought groceries, in that if something was in season that we weren't already growing she'd buy the local version of it. That being said, we had plenty of fruits and vegetables in our fridge year-round: there were imported tomatoes, greenhouse English cucumbers, Dole celery stalks, shrink-wrapped heads of lettuce, and waxy apples on hand whenever we wanted them. Seasonality was important, but it wasn't integral – otherwise we'd all have been slogging through the cold-weather months on potatoes, onions, and cabbage alone. And let's be real: no one-hundred-mile-dieter on earth is *really* doing that, no matter how vehemently the ideology calls for it.

But back to the peaches. Last August, just as peach season was hitting its juicy zenith, I took a detour on my usual route home to pick up a basket of the fuzzy stone fruits at a parking-lot farmers' market in Toronto's Annex neighbourhood. August is exactly the right time to visit a farmers' market in Ontario; all the best vegetables (unless you really love squash and turnips) are in season at local farms. I breezed past quarts of strawberries ($6) and three-litre baskets of cherries ($15), small bags of long green beans ($3.50), and artisanal loaves of bread ($8), before I found what I was looking for: a basket of fresh, almost-ripe, fuzzy-skinned, freestone Ontario peaches. Priced at $8.

Now, I'm not going to pretend that I don't have disposable income – nor that I don't have the tendency to, to put it mildly, waste a ton of money all the time (shout-out to my enormous collection of shoes I neither need nor wear nor fit into!). I'm lucky: I don't have children, without car payments or a mortgage my monthly bills are manageable, and I worked throughout my post-secondary education, which prevented me from taking out huge student loans. And even so, $8 for a bunch of fruit gives me pause; surely, in a city as large as Toronto, with food options as varied as the city is massive, I could get a better bargain?

I walked up the street a half block to a small fruit stand and found similar baskets of Ontario peaches marked down from $4.99 to $3.99. I don't know if they were ethical in any way. I do know that they were whole, real fruits, and that each and every one was delicious.

From a marketing perspective, it's almost in the best interest of farmers' markets to sell their products at a higher price than the large chain grocers: a higher cost to the consumer may (and often does) signal a premium product, whether or not the buyer is aware of the politics of small vs. industrial farming. The premium price point communicates the notion that farmers' market goods are worth more and, therefore, are better. Whatever *better* means here is highly subjective: to the *Food, Inc.* crowd, this might mean more sustainable (which, often as not, is simply to say organic and/or local.); to the consumer who's less inclined toward food politics, this could be interpreted to mean more nutritious, or more delicious, or simply more nostalgic – buying food directly from the farm seems like a novel callback to times of yore. Of course, the truth of the matter is that farmers' market produce *can* be all of the above. But it can also be none!

In Toronto, farmers' markets have multiplied exponentially in the ten-plus years since I first moved here. There are at least two farmers' markets every day of the week during growing season (spring to autumn), and at least one every other day during the cooler months. But take a look at where farmers' markets are situated, and a trend quickly reveals itself: with few exceptions, these pop-up bastions of artisanal goodness tend to set up shop in neighbourhoods that are affluent and/or gentrified; hip and cosmopolitan; or where there is daytime access to city tourism and a great deal of white-collar foot traffic. In Toronto's Annex, for instance, where I found those beautiful, pricey peaches, the average income (according to Canada's 2006 census) is $63,636; city-wide, the average income is more than $20,000 less than this. In other words: the farmers go where the money is. (This is also where people can afford to care about whether their fresh food is organic, and not just whether they can afford fresh food, full stop.)

And why not? Farming is hard work, and farmers deserve to make a financial return on the time and labour they invest. Surely a bit of the capitalist impulse is necessary to ensuring the continued existence of small family farms (as it always has been), just like any other business. The issue here isn't necessarily who growers are looking to access, but who's being shut out, and by which mechanisms.

Kelly Hodgins, an academic at the University of Guelph, focuses on how the price of 'ethical' food choices affects consumers across tax brackets. Hodgins, a British Columbia native, grew up farming. 'I was very much focused on the farming side of things, and supporting small farmers, and trying to create a local, Canadian food system that supports small farmers,' she says. 'Doing that really neglected food access for consumers.'

In researching her 2014 doctoral thesis, Hodgins looked not only at the high price margins of alternative food market spaces, such as farmers' markets, but she also conducted intensive interviews with the proprietors of these spaces –

vendors, and farmers themselves – to get a sense of what they believe to be barriers to access. The responses were too varied to list here. Among them was convenience: specialty stores and farmers' markets are open infrequently, keep odd hours, and are often simply not easy to get to for low-income individuals. The convenience factor, respondents said, also applied to the time it takes to cook food: one of Hodgins's interview subjects remarked that one can 'feed a family from scratch for three days, *if you wanna do it*' (emphasis his).

The issue here, as Hodgins notes, is the inaccurate assumption that shopping and cooking habits are typically framed as a matter of choosing to purchase fresh, organic foods over packaged ones, or to prepare one's own food from scratch instead of eating out. It's an especially egregious way of thinking when applied to low-income households, an extension of the age-old idea that if poor people would simply pull up their socks, work a bit harder, and maybe read a book or two, they'd be happier, healthier, and richer. Shaming the poor accomplishes nothing and is a handy way of covering the systems that perpetuate income inequality, and that idea – rooted in a bourgeois definition of financially anchored moral fortitude – is as wrong now as it ever was: a 2017 study by the University of Toronto research team PROOF found that those living in food-insecure households reported the same cooking abilities and menu-planning habits as those in higher income brackets. Desire for the organic peach is universal; access to the organic peach is not.

The lower-price fruits and vegetables available from chain grocery stores and big-box retailers are often the products of subsidized industrial agricultural system that perpetrates (and perpetuates) serious environmental and social ills. But they are fruits and vegetables all the same. And simply suggesting that individual consumers should choose to spend more money on food – whether to invest in better farming practices, to demonstrate through economic means that there ought to be more funding for alternative food-retail infrastructure, or both – assumes that such a choice exists. Alternative food markets "are sometimes touted as the silver bullet,' Hodgins says. 'But they're not. In fact, it's not a better food system than the conventional food system if it's excluding people.' Put another way: if a food system is not accessible, how can it *possibly* be sustainable?

On Saturday mornings during growing season, a cursory scroll of my Instagram feed reveals dozens of photos of 'market hauls': artfully laid-out mosaics of fresh-from-the-farm produce, meat, bread, and dairy. It's all very beautiful, but the immediate impression is not that these people are investing in a sustainable, grassroots, political movement – it just sort of looks like everyone is doin' it for the 'gram. Indeed, the farmers' market (and its adjacent farm-to-table ethos) feels more akin to an aesthetic than a movement. Posting geo-tagged photos from farm-to-table restaurants and artfully displaying an array of freshly procured ramps sends a message of affluence – living one's #bestlife is not always a world-changing endeavour. Besides, Williams-Sonoma doesn't sell $2,000 chicken coops because it's trying to save the world through locavorism; they sell them because locavorism is fashionable.

As far as trends go, mindfulness about our diets is a pretty good one to have gone mainstream. But as any fan of a stadium band who's been 'there from day one' will tell you, when things get big, people without much commitment to the cause can end up on the bandwagon – and they are very easily marketed to. For instance, the Loblaws chain of grocery stores in Canada sells a line of mass-produced but artisanal-looking foods under the brand – you guessed it – Farmer's Market™. If all you want is the look of locavorism, it's never been so easily attainable but so perilously close to meaninglessness.

Writing in the *Atlantic* in 2010, B. R. Meyers decried foodies as sanctimonious, entitled, elitist, out-of-touch snobs. Now everyone's a foodie – and, exasperatingly, that's a problem, too. Many farmers' markets in Toronto resemble upscale specialty grocers (and vice versa), with the customer base to match. 'As farm-to-table has slipped further away from the food movement and into the realms of foodie-ism and corporate marketing,' Los Angeles chef Andrea Reusing wrote for NPR's *The Salt* in June 2017, 'it is increasingly unhitched from the issues it is so often assumed to address.'

One of those issues is labour – and Reusing's use of the word *assumed* is key because, paradoxically, the local and sustainable-food movements have often overlooked the human factor of food production in favour of a focus on improving the well-being of animals and the health of the planet (for better or worse). If Canada's industrial food production system relies heavily on the work of low-paid migrant workers – and it does – many family farms in the country rely on the work of volunteers, interns, and seasonal apprentices paid in room and board: a 2014 study found that 65 per cent of the labour done on small- to medium-scale farms in Ontario is performed by unwaged individuals. It's not difficult to find people, particularly very young people, whose ideologies push them toward this kind of work – after all, learning to farm is learning how to save the planet, right? And since sustainable foodie-ism has never been so fashionable, what could be cooler than a summer spent harvesting organic peas and peaches? And this type of labour also helps farmers avoid adding costs to their overhead, which would in turn increase the cost of their products – which would in turn make their products even more exclusive than they already are. 'If we were to actually take away the volunteers and the unpaid interns,' Hodgins asks, 'how sustainable is that?'

Another large wedge between the average foodie and the moral, ethical, and environmental issues that the contemporary food movement was originated to address is the idea of 'clean eating.' This, to my knowledge and in my research, has not and likely will not have anything to do with food that's clean in the environmental sense, which is to say something closely approaching zero footprint or organic. It does mean organic, because clean eating is all about putting food into one's body that has the least amount of chemical intervention possible – however, it's not always this. Often it means detoxing with specious supplements, fasting, eating strange powders and guzzling odd serums, and probably reading *Goop*.

Clean eating is, to veer into snark for one second, an absolute plague on the food movement. The ideology behind the diet craze is far removed from the actual issues plaguing food and food production – it is also, in many ways, literally removed from food. In 2015, the *Elle* food diary of a woman (not unironically) named Amanda Chantal Bacon, who runs a juice bar in Los Angeles, went viral for reasons including – but not limited to – the fact that it discussed something called 'brain dust.' Brain dust, it behooves me to note, is not food. But this type of eating is not only popular, it is revered as the type of eating that gets one closer to transcendence or, at least, moral absolution; how can you even unintentionally eat food that isn't good for you when you aren't really eating any food at all?

It would be difficult to measure whether the ethos of eating 'clean' is of concern to the average farmers' market shopper, as that demographic has shifted from fringe environmentalists and food obsessives to include affluent yuppies for whom artisanal food products are potentially more a status symbol and marker of upward mobility than a form of grassroots protest. But this turn toward expensive produce as status symbol has certainly led to more brain-dust-type non-foods being shilled at farmers' markets, alongside artisanal tarts, hemp totes, and all the other types of non-food but tenuously food-adjacent stuff. This means more money being funnelled into alternative food markets on a consumer level, yes, which is positive, but as the local food movement moves farther from its ideological origins and closer to a mainstream business model, it may become easier to ignore and gloss over systemic issues that have prevented – and will continue to prevent – these food markets from becoming truly accessible, and more truly sustainable. Moon dust will not adequately address over-harvesting, climate change, and the need for green things in the diet of our children's children.

I love my August peaches first and foremost because they taste good. But since a fruit or vegetable at the height of its ripeness is usually a fruit or vegetable at its most nutritious – and my taste buds recognize this nutritiousness as deliciousness – I also subconsciously love my August peaches because they're good for me.

There is sufficient evidence and science to suggest that the shorter the chain of transportation of a fruit or vegetable from the plant to your plate, the greater the nutritional density will be in that fruit or vegetable. Hand in hand with this idea is the notion that the shorter the chain of transportation, the lesser the environmental impact.

In their 2012 book *The Locavore's Dilemma: In Praise of the 10,000-Mile Diet*, Toronto authors Pierre Desrochers (an associate professor of geography at the University of Toronto) and Hiroko Shimizu (who holds a master's in international public policy from the University of Osaka) suggest that this might not be the case. The book, to be clear, is a little extremist – the pair take literally the idea that locavores adhere to a 'hundred-mile diet' and that small family farmers shirk all modern technology and have instead reverted to pre-twentieth-century growing techniques. Overwhelmingly, this is not the case.

But there are facets of local food production that pale in comparison to larger-scale models when efficiency is factored in. If we consider food miles, is it more environmentally friendly, for instance, to transport a couple hundred heirloom tomatoes two hundred kilometres, once a week, to a farmers' market, where they will go to feed a couple dozen, or to pack a transport truck with hundreds of thousands of greenhouse tomatoes for three times the distance once a week, in order to feed thousands? Industrial farming operations carefully measure and mete out water, using only what they will need to grow what they know they can sell; this metric is far less precise on many small farms, resulting in wasted H_2O. Do large industrial farms put more energy – in manpower as well as fossil fuels – into growing food than small family farms, if you measure output in calories?

These questions don't always have clear answers and, when they have answers at all, they don't always weigh in favour of local producers who provide food to alternative food markets. Efficiency isn't the be-all and end-all in measures of sustainability as far as food production is concerned – in many ways, the opposite is true, since the desire for more efficient, infinitely scalable industrial food production is largely why we're in the mess we're currently in with our food systems worldwide. But it's a significant part of the puzzle, particularly when you're at the farmers' market, considering why an eight-dollar basket of peaches is worth eight dollars.

To me, farmers' markets are important. I get pleasure from giving money, when I can, to small businesses, and farmers are no exception. I find the produce more visually appealing and, sometimes, more delicious. The increased prevalence of farmers' markets says, to me, that some needle has been pushed forward in our national conversation about the detrimental effects of industrial food production, and that there are more people – for whatever reason – investing in change.

Many, if not all, of the farmers working their stalls at the market are strongly committed to what they believe to be the most responsible farming practices, for what they believe to be the most altruistic reasons. The local-food movement began out of a desire to have an alternative to large-scale industrial food production practices – and it is a hugely pleasurable alternative. But it's not a one-size-fits-all *solution* to unsustainable food systems.

The farmers' market approach to shopping and growing is actually not a completely viable approach for all farmers either – farmers are struggling. According to a December 2017 story in the *Guardian* by reporter Debbie Weingarten, farmers are killing themselves at record rates; the alternative-food movement has not significantly affected how easy, or sustainable, or lucrative it is to be a farmer. The idea that this has happened is maybe true in certain pockets, but it is largely a convenient myth spread by those whose Gospel of Good Food depends on perpetuating the idea that decades of farm-to-tabling has made a difference. It has – but only ideologically. There are simply too many outside factors pushing on farmers – urbanization, unpredictable weather patterns, cheap imports, rising land costs – for a bunch of people with nice ideas and the money to buy an organic squash once a week to have effected any salient change. How do we help these farmers? This book is not an answer to that question, but we nonetheless ought to stop pretending the question has already been addressed by our Instagrammed baskets of strawberries.

If the classic farmers' market is unsustainable, what does sustainable, farmer-friendly food retail look like, in an urban context? One answer might be Fresh City Farms, in Toronto.

My first meeting with Hannah Hunter, Fresh City's farm manager, took place on a cool, windy, mid-October afternoon. This is an important detail, because our conversation occurred on the two-acre plot that comprises Fresh City, in Downsview Park. I was actually meant to be there a day sooner but, being the type of person who's meticulously organized about my possessions but chronically forgetful about my appointments, I'd flatly gotten the day wrong. Hannah doesn't seem to mind. 'I'm here pretty much every day anyway,' she says, shaking my hand in the greenhouse that serves as the gateway to Fresh City Farms' actual acreage. Hannah, wearing a plaid button-down and with her hair gathered into a messy top knot, looks every inch the modern-day farmer – because, of course, she is one. She quickly guides me out the back door and into the biting wind.

Though late in the season, there are still plenty of delicate, leafy greens growing and, uncharacteristic for October, whole vines of tomatoes that have yet to ripen. I even notice a few eggplants still hanging heavy off their stems, plus onions and the kales and chards and other robust greens that are more typical of autumn than their salady cousins. Weather-wise, 2017 was an irregular season for agriculture – in case you've forgotten: the summer was cold and wet, followed by a sudden shock of extreme heat in late September, which, for one thing, led to fresh-off-the-vine, fresh-from-the-farm tomatoes well into October). Hunter explains how the late-season bounty is unusual, and adds that it's hard to know exactly what constitutes 'usual' on a farm this new (Fresh City was established in 2011). Just like on conventional, country farms, every season brings a new set of variables that are completely out of Hannah's control: pests, extreme weather patterns resulting from climate change, heavy rains, no rains, and, as is typical anywhere in the City of Toronto, the occasional wily raccoon.

Fresh City Farms is divided by a sloping path: on one side is the stuff that Hannah and her small staff grow for distribution to their CSA subscribers; on the other are 'member farms,' which are plots slightly larger than conventional community garden plots but significantly smaller than farms. The growing area of Fresh City occupies two of its six acres, with about half of that split among about twenty member growers. There's no structural divide between Fresh City's growing space and member farmers' growing space, but the difference is obvious: where Fresh City's produce grows in tidy rows, member gardens tend to run a bit more amok, with wildflowers and weeds interspersed among food-producing plants often allowed to run a bit wild. They're functional gardens, of course, but they're obviously non-commercial. That being said, on these smallish plots, regular folks can experiment with crops large enough to be *used* for commercial purposes, should they choose: some, Hannah tells me, sell their bounty at farmers' markets, if the harvest proves large enough. Others use their plots for education, like one member farmer who conducts reiki – an alternative healing method that focuses on energy distribution through the body – right in her garden.

Fresh City's member-farmer model is a bit of an experiment in recontextualizing what it means to be a farmer, in a giant city – in this case, Toronto. Fresh City Farms blends city and country, and then gets creative with what this hybridization might mean, and might accomplish: what does it look like to reconnect with nature, when we allow cities to be part of nature (and vice versa)?

But with only twenty member farmers, plus a limited growing season and minimal acreage, Fresh City's experiment in urban agriculture is just that: more of an experiment (and a valuable one!) in viewing cities as food-producers than a panacea for the issues plaguing food access in urban centres. 'Generally, I think that urban farming, the purpose of it, is to have people understand better what agriculture looks like, and for people to be able to access more space to grow their own food, if that's important to them,' says Hunter. 'I don't think Toronto-grown food is going to take over the supermarket.' But Fresh City has taken moves to *supplant* the supermarket itself: a couple months after I visited the farm, it took over a bricks-and-mortar space in downtown Toronto, with the intention to convert it to a food market selling the types of items typically available to Fresh City subscribers, as well as its own Downsview Park– grown produce. A second Fresh City Farm market opened shortly thereafter, with plans for a third in the works.

At Downsview, there is something alien about traipsing among rows of rainbow chard while facing gridlock traffic and a massive gas station billboard. It's a visual experience more suited to the parking lot of a big-box store than the acreage of an organic (though not certifiably so) farmland – if you can even call it farmland. But Fresh City is part of a growing global coterie of urban farms: small-scale growing operations that are transforming land – and other infra- structure – in urban centres into food-producing operations. Canada has North America's largest such farm: Sole Food, a Vancouver outfit that, in early 2017, began moving to a disused area in the city's former Olympic Village.

If the actual, literal opposite of *city* is *country*, its spiritual opposite is *farm*. We tend to differentiate city living from country living logistically and, as it relates to food, in a sort of moral sense: country folk, we think, have a stronger connection to and therefore reverence for their food; city people think food comes from a box – or from an Uber driver – and don't give a second thought to its provenance, the human labour that went into its production, and the environmental cost of its consumption. Either that or there's an urban, affluent prioritization of food with foodie cachet – your farm-to-table, organic, line-caught stuff – without a real understanding of or concern with what the production process means, outside of the fact that it's buzzword-friendly. And while I say I grew up in a city – which, for all intents and purposes, I did: I have lived in Toronto since age eighteen, and what kind of growing up really happens before that point, anyway? – I always had access to at least a fraction of the education that rural North Americans tend to think their urban counterparts are lacking: a front-row look at what it takes to grow food, at least for a family of four, and how good that food tastes when it's on the table. Sort of the best of both worlds, but without any livestock – even though my mother would have always loved to have chickens. So, almost the best of both worlds.

For a while, in my mid-twenties, I had a small community garden plot in a large park in downtown Toronto. I wanted to start growing my own vegetables, partly because I missed eating fresh, sun-ripened tomatoes in the summer. But it was largely because I'd begun shopping at farmers' markets and learning a bit more about sustainable food systems – and I thought literally getting my hands dirty was the best possible way to prove, to myself and to others, that I was a person who Truly Cared About Food, Because I Grew It Myself. This was in adherence to the teachings of the prophets of good food who I'd been listening to at the time – Pollan, Bittman, et al. Their mantras and proclamations boiled down to the importance of reconnecting with our food and simplifying what we ate. Roughly two years into my tenure living away from my parents' house, my all-too-frequent consumption of processed, packaged, and ready-made food was beginning to weigh on me – morally and literally. Willing to forgive myself for my junk-food experimentation but wanting to change my ways, I seized on the opportunity to swing the pendulum as far as possible in the other direction: no longer would I be eating bags of chips and three-hundred-gram chocolate bars for dinner! Instead, I would grow – and eat – vegetables!

The wait list for the community plot was a couple years long, and by the time I'd been given the space, I'd forgotten I'd signed up for it. And once I actually started growing things, I started forgetting to stop by the plot more often than I popped in – resulting in overgrown cucumbers, lettuce gone to seed, and tomatoes that either got stolen, eaten by raccoons, or killed by my negligence (it was a dry summer). As anyone who's ever tried to pick up a high-intensity fitness regimen after years of couch-potatoing will tell you, lifestyle changes need to be incremental to be sustainable. The all-or-nothing approach, applied to food or fitness or friendship or just about anything else human beings experience in their day-to-day lives, is often a recipe for failure. And so, my lettuce died, and I went back to hitting the Lay's – but now with an even stronger sense of moral ineptitude, having literally killed things in my quest for foodie absolution.

Hannah Hunter is partly right when she says it's impor-tant for urban dwellers to understand where their food comes from. A greater connection to food fosters a greater appreciation and, by association, a greater respect – though, largely, this respect is understood in sustainable-food circles to mean a desire to buy local, organic, artisanal products, with little regard for how accessible these products actually are. And, anyway, city people understand food just fine:

that's why all the most successful nose-to-tail, foraged-menu restaurants are in major metropolises, right? But city dwellers are not farmers and community garden plots and backyards are both luxuries as urban density intensifies. The concept of urban farming allows for an interesting levelling of the playing field, in that it brings a fraction of the farm onto a fraction of the city, albeit in a way that is accessible only to a fraction of the people.

Fresh City Farms is even more interesting – the acreage I toured is only part of the story; the farm's CSA members get food from Fresh City year-round, because it sources tons of product – from dairy to pantry goods to meat, bread, and seafood – from farmers and producers within the city, and well beyond. Fresh City Farms meets its customers in the middle, with an awareness that people want alternative ways to shop for the foods they might not be able to morally justify – imported fruit, for instance. Fresh City does the legwork of finding the most responsible way to bring that food across the border. 'It's an alternative to getting that nice produce during the summer months, and the rest of the year you have to go to Loblaws,' Hunter tells me. 'Or you have to go to Loblaws, anyway, because you can't shake those lemons and apples.'

And for Fresh City Farms, 'responsibly' means a lot of things – sometimes organic, sometimes local. The important – and remarkable – thing about its business model is the flexibility: Fresh City understands that an urban demographic is a complex customer base with complex needs; it strives to serve them in the most dynamic way possible.

If we want to get people in cities closer – literally – to their food, we'll need to embrace this kind of flexibility. Adhering to a Manichean divide between cities and farmers makes it easier to suggest that the most sustainable food furor is in investing more money in preserving farms the way we imagine they always were. Likewise, city folk, like planners, developers, and architects, argue for density – human density – in the urban arena, accommodating transit, walkability, and accessibility, but not actual sustenance. In other words, keep the farms in the country and the highrises in the city. But with urban populations growing – the world is hurtling toward 70 per cent urbanization by 2050, the same year the global population is projected to hit nine billion – and farmable land growing ever more scarce, it might be time for the twain to meet.

In her seminal 1961 book *The Death and Life of Great American Cities*, renowned urbanist Jane Jacobs presents cities as problems of 'organized complexity': 'Cities...do not exhibit *one* problem in organized complexity, which if understood explains all... [T]hey are "interrelated into an organic whole."'

Urbanism, or the study of the interactions between humans and the cities they live in – and how those cities are designed – is an important piece of the sustainable-food puzzle. In 2014, a paper by NYU Marron Institute researchers Brandon Fuller and Paul Romer projected that, by 2210, nearly 87 per cent of the the world's population would live in cities, largely in developing nations. That's 9.8 billion people calling urban centres their home. If we continue to depend on the country and the country alone for food the way we do now – which is to say: through a combination of environmentally taxing industrialized means of production and small-scale, resource-intense small organic operations – the environmental toll will be extraordinary. But as urban planners grapple with the most functional ways to accommodate growing density in city centres, while planning for cities that are humane and livable, it would make sense to begin considering cities not only places for people, businesses, and buildings, but also for food.

Start with the city park, where you might put a community garden. The use of the park, Jacobs writes, is designated by the design of the park, and the design of the park depends on who uses the park, which itself depends 'on uses of the city outside the park itself.' Parks in many ways serve to mitigate these 'uses of the city,' in that they provide green space, recreation, and respite – parks are often miniature oases, tiny green bastions against the towering concrete and hot pavement of the city. The existence of the city park acknowledges a base, deeply human desire to, essentially, be outside. It would make sense for city parks to also mitigate against the dearth of access to farm-fresh food that exists within urban centres – to acknowledge that one 'use of the city outside the park itself' is to replace green space with grey infrastructure, and to divorce residents from food production.

But while government bodies include individuals who are responsible for urban green spaces, and others overseeing agriculture, there's no such thing as a Ministry of Urban Agriculture. At the policy level, farms (where we grow food) and cities (where we build buildings) are also fundamentally divorced. Retrofitting major metropolises as food-producing ecosystems has not, in large part, been factored into what Jacobs would call the 'organic whole' of the city. The term *vertical farming*, at present, is used to mean shelves of plants that are stacked on top of one another and grown indoors – but imagine an evolution that saw that phrase come to stand in for farming that simply *takes place* in our increasingly vertical cities. There's actually a name for this: it's called agritecture.

Waterwheel Farms is one example of a vertical farm that fits the standard definition. Technically, it's not a farm at all: it's an aquaponics outfit, using the waste produced by fish to grow leafy greens in an entirely closed-loop ecosystem. Aquaponics is one of the two primary types of vertical farming one might find in major cities; the other is hydroponics, which uses nutrients distilled into a water solvent to grow plants indoors, without the use of soil. Aquaponics allows for faster plant maturation (lettuces grow in twenty days using aquaponics rather than sixty using hydroponics), but both methods of vertical farming allow for the year-round, weather-irrespective growing of produce.

When I visited on a late summer afternoon, Waterwheel Farms was still in the proof-of-concept stage: Alex Wheeler, Waterwheel's proprietor, was touring visitors through his open-house set-up in a warehouse in downtown Toronto, where he'd assembled two small towers, each about five metres high, growing soilless, fish-waste-fed bunches of lettuce. Because aquaponics systems are efficient, produce fresh product in precious little time, and require relatively little indoor space (depending on how much one wants to grow, of course), Wheeler told me he sees a huge opportunity for vertical farming operations like his (and for his in particular) to open up shop in cities, where space is scarce, and also in food deserts, to provide fresh, local produce to people who otherwise have little access to any food, let alone the fresh kind.

A few months after the open house, Waterwheel secured a larger warehouse space just outside of the city, where

Wheeler plans to fill eight thousand square feet – two thousand square feet of actual floor area, multiplied by four vertically stacked shelves of aquaponic shelving – with kale, arugula, dill, and other lettuces and herbs. Conservatively, he estimates the shelving will hold twenty thousand individual plants at any one time. If those individual plants grow in twenty days, Waterwheel could sell around 365,000 plants a year – which might be a bigger deal if we weren't talking about lettuce, sold at wholesale prices to restaurants, from a high-rent warehouse near Toronto. Wheeler does things on the cheap – Waterwheel doesn't use much industry-specific equipment but opts instead for hardware-store barrels and piping – but the start-up cost is nevertheless prohibitive. All that is to say, it's hard to eke out a sustainable living on fish-poop-fed arugula alone. And for all the condo developments and density projects underway in cities such as Toronto, few – if any – are integrating vertical farming infrastructure into their planning.

It's not just start-up capital and lack of municipal prioritization that holds vertical farming back from being more widely adopted. Vertical farming is controversial, too, but in a very particular way: in 2017, the United States Department of Agriculture (USDA) and the National Organic Standards Board voted to allow hydroponic growing outfits to use organic certification – a vote that enraged traditional organic farmers in the US, who believe that soil integrity is the key to determining whether a food is organic (and, remember: hydroponics is soilless). While the vote signalled progress for indoor farmers hoping to market their goods to the organics-loving audience, the backlash served as a reminder that, when it comes to food production, the divide between so-called traditional methodology and technological solutions is stark and slightly myopic: hydroponic lettuces check off so many boxes on the sustainability card – they're pesticide-free; not very resource-intensive, considering how little land they require; vegan; and definitely local. The mere introduction of twentieth-century innovation, however, makes them *vegetablis non grata*.

At the Arrell Food Institute, Evan Fraser believes that, as the global population increases, urban solutions such as vertical farming will become all the more important – and, perhaps, more widely adopted. 'The technologies have changed so rapidly,' he says, 'that, I suspect, instead of importing lettuce from California we'll be buying vertical farmed lettuce from the outskirts of Toronto, and that vertical farm will be located close to a manufacturing facility where there's a lot of waste heat and waste carbon dioxide, and it will use summer light and summer temperatures where appropriate and the rest of the year it will be doing LED lighting and hydroponics.' In case you got a bit lost there, that's a vertical farming solution that also solves for a bit of industrial pollution, and cuts down on shipping cost and its associated environmental impact.

Fraser points out that, while we technically do have enough food to feed the world right now, what that means is that we have enough calories; there are only three or four servings of fruits and vegetables per person on the planet today. If the future of food means producing better food with better means for more people using fewer resources, it might be prudent to start with high-density warehoused urban lettuce.

In 2016, the BBC released the documentary TV series *Planet Earth II*, the follow-up to its immensely popular *Planet*

Earth from 2010. Unlike its predecessor, *Planet Earth II* dedicated an entire episode to an altogether unnatural set of ecosystems: cities.

After dedicating ample airtime to ways in which animals and humans have come to coexist in urban environments (part of which, to my delight and the delight of some of my friends, focused on the raccoons of Toronto), *Planet Earth II* turned its lens to Singapore, where a futuristic series of structures are not simply being adapted to by wild flora and fauna: they are, instead, inviting that flora and fauna in.

Two million trees have been planted in Singapore in the last forty-five years; the city, narrator David Attenborough notes, is now 'richer in species than any other in the world.' Singapore's Gardens by the Bay, in particular, almost defy description: they're 'supertrees,' forty-five-metre-high metal structures covered in plant life designed to attract birds and insects. The 'trees' themselves collect rainwater, generate solar power, act as air-venting ducts for conservatories located nearby, and provide shade for human visitors below. The Gardens by the Bay do not actually grow any food – these are not vertical farms, per se, though the plants that grow from each supertree provide food and shelter for animals. But they are an extremely effective example of how urban planning can allow for the unconventional integration of plant growth – for our benefit and the benefit of our non-human neighbours.

Back in North America, the integration of plant and human life is not so thoughtful, or so seamless. The hydroponics-as-organics debate was that heated, passionate, and at times personal for old-school farming advocates. The debate was also kind of, well, weird: 'Most Americans probably don't think about hydroponic farms (which grow plants inside soilless greenhouses in trays of nutrient solution), and aquaponic farms (which marry hydroponics and aquaculture – or farmed fish and other aquatic organisms – to produce plants and fish crops) when they picture an organic farm,' Joe Fassler and Kate Cox, of the non-profit US publication *New Food Economy*, wrote.

> That's because we often associate the *word* 'organic' with a more traditional, pastoral vision of crops grown under the open air, perhaps accompanied by a red farmhouse and some cows grazing in the background. And while that vision is far from what organic – now a more than $50 billion industry in the United States alone – has become, many organic farmers, especially the older, more traditional sort, who pioneered and advocated for the certification in the first place, want to make sure that certification extends only to this more traditional interaction with a plot of land.

But why? Are those older, more traditional sorts of farmers not missing the forest for the supertrees? These days, Fassler and Cox suggest, organic certification is barely more than a marketing term; sure, there are farms out there that are *actually* organic, whatever that means – but the consumer isn't going to do the legwork to figure out if they are. And they shouldn't have to. An organic label is simply a tool to attract consumers to a product that is, in theory, more sustainable than something that's hugely processed and industrialized. 'There's the organic ethos,' writes Tamar Haspel, the *Washington Post* food columnist, 'and then there's the USDA organic certification program, and they're not the same. One is about farming ecologically, and the other is about making money by farming ecologically.' The red-barn farmers should only care about the former, right?

The premise of organic certification, Haspel writes, is that farms 'must "demonstrate that they are protecting natural resources, conserving biodiversity, and using only approved substances." It's a broad definition, and hydroponic and aquaponic farms have, so far, successfully made the case that they meet it.' And while a few red-barn farmers might genuinely object to the idea that a soilless growing operation can go organic on some sort of moral principle, the objection likely boils down to something an awful lot more cynical being masked as something ethical, altruistic, and good: 'one group of farmers who make money from the certification arguing that another group shouldn't have the same chance,' Haspel says.

It troubles me that any definition of good food would exclude outfits whose growing ideologies and goals are, like those of Waterwheel Farms, altruistic and noble. It troubles me further that, at the root of these definitions and debates is economic competition: something that should and always will exist in any industry, yes, but who does it serve to say that real food can only be produced in one way – a way whose methodologies are firmly entrenched in the early twentieth century? And then to stonewall the competition?

And yet I understand the protectiveness: the nostalgia of old-timey farm values is a potent marketing tool that's not always used to sell foods that fit old-timey farm values. So let's just do away with those values altogether! They don't seem to be serving anyone. More than that, they're dangerous: the world is a changed place, where density, volatile climate patterns, and rampant urbanization have largely decimated the legitimate existence of the traditional farm, which has in turn threatened the livelihood of the traditional farmer. But instead of looking at change as a threat – or as a crisis – why not view it as an opportunity? Let's replace traditional farming values with new ones that are inclusive not only of farmers, but of the new economic conditions that require their continued existence. Now more than ever, the world needs people who understand how to grow food. Farmers ought to be empowered with new tools, but this requires shifting to a mindset that recognizes those tools as empowering, not dangerous.

3

Kill Your Idylls

The diligent farmer plants trees, of which he himself will never see the fruit.

– Cicero, approximately 30 BCE

KRAMER: 'Kurt, taste these eggs.'
KURT: 'Uh, no. I only eat cage-free, farm-fresh.'
KRAMER: 'Yes. These are sweatshop eggs!'

– *Seinfeld*, 1996

W ill Bergmann stood in front of attendees at the 2017 Terroir Symposium and wished death upon the family farm.

For the uninitiated, Terroir is an annual gathering of food industry professionals of all sorts – from writers and researchers to farmers, butchers, bakers, and chefs – who, for roughly $300 a head, convene for a day of seminars, finger foods, and, of course, networking. (I attended Terroir for four consecutive years, thrice as a member of the media and once as a member of the symposium's organizing committee.) The idea of the event is, loosely, the exchange of ideas – but, given the steep ticket cost, those ideas typically reach only a rarefied audience. It is as exclusive as anything else that opts for 'symposium' over, say, 'conference.'

With the foodie elitism that accompanies a $300 networking ticket comes elitist foodie ideology, in the form of…well, in this case, it's right there in the name: an obsession with *terroir*, the French oenophilic word we use to discuss how the micro-conditions of a geographical region result in perhaps minutely perceptible differences in how the food that grows there tastes. Everything that happens at Terroir is underpinned by an almost fanatical adherence to the idea that real food comes, literally, from the earth. So lobbing a death wish on family farms – which, at Terroir, mainly means the small, pastoral, picturesque, idealized operations that supply heritage hens and specialized produce to the customers and establishments who can afford to buy it – was unexpected, to say the least. It was also thrilling.

Bergmann is himself a farmer. Bergmann Farms, just outside of Winnipeg, is a medium-size operation growing mainly grains, plus enough organic produce to supply a couple hundred CSA subscriptions. He's a family farmer, too: his father and uncle ran Bergmann Farms before he did. What he was wishing death upon wasn't the idea that multiple generations can make their livelihoods working the same plots of land, but the way that relying on tradition and nostalgia makes farming today harder and more wasteful than it has to be.

As part of a panel titled 'Growing Forward,' Bergmann was at Terroir to explain, advocate for, and discuss precision farming, the technology-led, newish approach to agriculture that positions GPS analysis, specialized software, and smart-technology-enabled machines at the forefront of the next agricultural revolution. His core message – that the old-fashioned way of growing food isn't sustainable – was a fresh diversion from the usual warm-and-fuzzy farm-to-table platitudes of Terroir. Frankly, it was the most interested I'd ever been in one of the symposium's panel discussions, which typically preach to the choir.

A lot of other people were engaged, too, but not because they were picking up what Bergmann – or Nancy Tout, the head of regulatory and biological assessment for genetically modified seed giant Syngenta, who was seated beside him – was putting down. During a Q&A following the panel discussion, which also included Vancouver chef and sustainable seafood advocate Ned Bell, a self-described family farmer approached the mic and loudly lambasted Bergmann for his declarations. Others accused Tout, who briefly discussed the importance of including science and technology in conversations about agricultural sustainability, of mere corporate shillery. (For what it's worth, nobody seemed to have any issues with Bell.)

The panel's idea, basically, was to assemble three essential links in the food chain of the future – a scientist, farmer, and chef – and have them explain why their respective approaches to food sustainability are complementary. But what happened was a tense, heady blend of corporate distrust, misunderstanding, backpedalling, and apologia. If it were to be measured by its stated goals, the panel was an utter failure. But that was because, I think, the Terroir audience is so heavily (if not financially) invested in the idea that the most moral approach to food, in the future, is the slow-food, farm-fresh, all-organic approach. Bergmann offered an alternative – actually, a middle ground – that smacked of heresy.

Five months later, Will Bergmann texted me a picture of his combine.

I got the photo during a call with Will, as he was riding through his fields in Manitoba. If we hadn't been in the middle of talking about it, I would have had no idea what was in the image he sent: it's partly a rectangle chopped into hundreds of smaller rectangles – some green, some yellow, a few red, and a couple purple. There's a green circle over a grid of about eight rectangles off to the right; to the left, there's a legend, with numerical values assigned to each colour. Left of that are two icons that look like hourglasses, and two green-and-white-striped squares (one of which contains a question mark) sitting below the word 'Combine.' I was in Toronto looking at what Will was looking at about an hour outside of Winnipeg: a live, GPS-created map of his entire farm, colour-coded by crop yield.

Precision farming, the technique Bergmann uses, has a lot to do with GPS; it's these satellite-created measurements and readings that allow farmers to do things in a way that's, well, way more precise. On Bergmann's farm, this means a little satellite receiver attached to, say, a tractor, with a black box attached to its steering wheel. 'On the little black box,' Bergmann explains, 'you adjust for whatever width of implement you are pulling – a forty-foot cultivator, for instance – and then it would make you drive in straight lines that are exactly forty feet apart.' This seems simple – and kind of boring – but the implications are significant: first and foremost, there's no overlap. 'My dad and my uncle had machines that were twenty-five feet wide and we were overlapping one foot, at least, for every pass,' Bergmann says. 'Twenty-five passes later, and you've done an entire width of your machine.' For the farmer, this inefficiency would mean one pass of dispersed seed or fertilizer that's 100 per cent waste. It also means one unnecessary pass's worth of burned fossil fuels, whenever that machine – or any machine like it – is driven anywhere, at any time.

The bigger deal, though, is what was in the text-message picture. The definition of precision farming is evolving, but it is at its core the idea of doing more with less – or, more accurately, *growing* more *on* less. It's an agricultural best practice that's as old as agriculture itself – farmers for all of history have, one way or another, measured yield against weather patterns, variances in soil type and chemical composition, and the amount of fertilizer used (or not used), among other variables, to learn what grows best, under what conditions, and with what assistance. With precision machines, however, these measurements are taken on a basis determined by individual farmers (usually daily), then overlaid day over day, month over month, and year over year, to eventually paint a complete portrait comprising soil type, water output, fertilizer and chemical use, and yield, which will allow farmers to make decisions for the future of their crops that are rooted in remarkably rich, fail-safe data sets.

'Now,' Bergmann says, 'we recognize the historical data on our fields, of the spots that are consistently yielding more and consistently yielding less, and we can analyze that, and ask why. In the Red River Valley, where we are, that's generally a moisture issue: in the bottom of the ditches, it's generally not going to yield as well. So, for instance, we can look at that map and say, okay, we need to make a drainage plan on our field to make sure that the low spots that are consistently yielding less have drains. We take that GPS technology and cross it with laser levelling, and dig ditches that can be as small as a one-inch slope, for a mile.'

Measuring all this stuff to hyper-hyper-minute levels of accuracy is difficult, if not impossible, to do on medium- to large-scale farms, which has led not only to smaller yields than are technically possible (though to what degree has heretofore gone unknown), but also to significant margins of loss. Take, for instance, high-clearance crop sprayers. 'It's a necessary thing for us to do to use pesticides and herbicides,' Bergmann says. 'They're used minimally, but they need to be used.' His sprayer sprays ninety feet wide at a time, and has two tires on each side that are fourteen inches wide. The sprayer drives in a straight line across the land, with its tires touching the ground for twenty-eight inches every ninety feet. 'And it's driving across the crop,' Bergmann points out, 'so we're trampling that crop and losing 2 per cent of what we've planted.' He notes that farmers in Britain – who have much less land for their crops – have mapped everything on their farm to specific sizes and dimensions. When they're seeding, they have left out rows in exactly the width of the tires on the sprayer that they plan to use later on. 'Why aren't we doing that?' Bergmann says. 'Because it's a manageable loss. We do things sometimes just because this is how we've always done them. It takes a lot of advocacy, and sometimes it takes generations, to make change on farms.'

These days, however, even in North America, the mitigation of waste is key, and farmland is an endangered species: we're allocating more land to residences, to accommodate a growing population, and real-estate developers have much deeper pockets than farmers and family-farming advocates. The idea of growing more on less has never been so urgent. And never mind producing more: how can we continue to justify the loss of 2 per cent of a given crop when we have the technology to prevent it – and how much more food will we end up with if we *do* prevent this loss, every year, on every farm across the country?

For answers, we might look to the Dutch. In the Netherlands, the implementation of precision farming technologies (which advance from Bergmann-style GPS-assisted machinery to drones), among other technological methods and innovations, has led the country's farmers to some remarkable milestones in output efficiency. According to a September 2017 *National Geographic* story about farming in the Netherlands, the Dutch have over the past two decades cut their water input by 90 per cent and massively increased their agricultural output in the process. It's not all due to precision agricultural practices. But for a country with a population density of 488 people per kilometre squared (by contrast, Canada has 3.7 people per kilometre squared), this is a remarkable agricultural feat.

The next wave, Bergmann says, is seeders and planters that aren't just planting one seed or one type of fertilizer, but rather multiple types of seed and fertilizer that are specific to specific parts of a farmer's field, and can be applied at different rates, depending on what the yield-mapping data indicates. This is known as variable-rate technology. But here, even he is out of the game. 'No one in Canada will use them,' he says. 'The technology is too expensive.' At least for the foreseeable future.

Joe Dales, co-founder of the agricultural news service farms.com, comes from a farming family. He also has a background in marketing and sales, and more than twenty-five years' experience in the agribusiness sector. He says that one of the issues facing precision agriculture in Canada exists at the corporate level, as software providers, machine suppliers, and seed growers learn to work together. He points out, though, that farming is a capital-intensive business, precision or not. 'What's expensive,' he says, 'is if it doesn't work.'

And if it does work, not all the benefits are immediate. The results of avoiding overlap and reducing chemical output are easy to see on the farmer's bottom line, but it takes years to get the sort of rich soil data that Will Bergmann has access to via his GPS-equipped machines; then it'll take another few years of data analysis to figure out the best way to apply machine learning to his field. But if it works, there's money to be made: research into the economics of precision farming, cited by *National Geographic*, found that small farms that implemented precision technologies saw an average gross annual benefit of US$11,000; for mid-size farms, this amount was $26,000; for large farms of 2,400 acres or more, the amount was $39,000. Higher yield, lower cost, less farmer fatigue, and a healthier bottom line: how is everybody not using this stuff?

Putting aside the issue of cost, one answer to that question might come from thinking back to Bergmann's appearance at Terroir. Precision farming, in spite of its being basically an evolved, high-tech version of farming principles that have existed since the dawn of agriculture, is a mechanized, newfangled, science-heavy, semi-industrial process – it looks, in other words, to be in the same league as other types of away-from-the-earth food-producing practices that gimlet-eyed food purists consider immoral and bad. At Terroir, Bergmann's delivery may have been a bit hyperbolic, but months later – when I saw him speak on a future-of-food-focused panel at the Expo for Design, Innovation and Technology alongside an organic-food evangelist – the reception was similar: a skepticism, if not pious dismissal, of his idea that innovative farming technology is not only important, but integral.

It's not likely that all of the technologies offered under the umbrella of precision agriculture are practical to all farms. Remember: a small farm, in the context of precision farming, is defined as around 800 acres. A 2016 USDA study found that those who adopt precision agriculture have farms that average 480 acres larger than those who don't — this is largely because the more sophisticated equipment is a massive capital expenditure that small farms simply can't shoulder. But also, because the issues of inefficiency solved by precision ag simply don't require the intervention of drones, smart combines, and sophisticated soil-mapping technology on smaller farms, small plots are easy to study, map, and learn from the old-fashioned way (which is where precision agriculture got all its ideas in the first place). Your farmers' market CSA box, in other words, might not require the efficiency of variable rate seeding. And if you consider super-small family farms and hyper-local alternative food markets to be the *only* future of food, precision agriculture might seem like a whole lot of corporate bluster.

In fairness, for all the good it does (and promises to do), precision agriculture raises a uniquely modern concern that is, relative to the lifespan of human-led agricultural practices, new on the farm: data privacy. Agricultural data is hugely sensitive, because it's economically valuable: as Jody L. Ferris points out in the 2017 *Minnesota Journal of Law, Science & Technology*, information about yield and output of important crops such as corn, soy, and wheat can be used to speculate on massive facets of the food market, and to influence trading activity on the stock market. This is to say nothing of general concerns about data privacy and ownership that also pervade the collection of information via precision agriculture, such as ownership of names and addresses (in this case, via precise GPS coordinates), or whether information can be hacked and accessed by competitors (in this case, other users of precision farming technology) to influence and assist their own businesses.

This concern is not going unaddressed. The USDA-supported Open Ag Data Alliance is dedicated to, among other things, developing secure APIs that will enable farmers to store their data in trusted cloud providers. OADA asserts that all farmers should have exclusive ownership over the data produced on their farms by their precision agriculture-enabled machines. Another organization, AgGateway, is also partly devoted to the development of best practices for data privacy. AgGateway is a consortium of companies, however, many of whom have substantial investments in precision agriculture tech: chief among them, Deere and Monsanto.

In fact – and perhaps unsurprisingly – Monsanto is one of the key players in precision ag. The Climate Corporation (a subsidiary of Monsanto) sells software called FieldView that does the whole precision gamut, from GPS soil mapping to variable rate seeding to data analysis. They're partnered with some of the other leaders in precision ag, including Deere – another company whose pivot to precision tech is logical, considering the prominent role it has long played in farming overall. But the scale and scope is fascinating (particularly to those who, like me, associate kelly-green John Deere tractors with a particular brand of agrarian earthiness).

In early 2017, Deere spent $305 million to acquire Blue River Technology, a tech start-up based in Santa Clara, California. Monsanto Growth Ventures is among Blue River's investors: the company shelled out just over $17 million during Blue River's Series B funding. The whole thing looks a whole lot more Silicon Valley than Old

MacDonald, because it is: precision-agriculture tech promises to make life easier, more efficient, and more comfortable by taking manual processes and automating them.

So, how is this not the Big Brother of agribusiness? Dales and Bergmann both pointed out that one of the most significant potential impacts of precision agriculture is its positive impact on the environment.

Historically, farmers of medium- to large-scale crops – the kind that can best utilize precision practices – have tried to grow the same thing, in the same place, year over year. Using precision data, farmers can learn what grows best in what areas, and adjust their planting accordingly. This might mean that, using science, precision farmers may essentially adopt the tenets of biodynamic farming, allowing the land to guide their input, and not the other way around. Farming would become proactive rather than reactive, eliminating undue stress on farmland and the surrounding ecosystems at large.

Imagine: Monsanto-led sustainable agriculture. It sounds crazy. It also sounds like a fantasy, so long as the purism around ideas of good food remains prevalent.

The introduction of complex technologies onto the old-fashioned farm is, naturally, heading the same direction the introduction of technology to all industries has gone: toward automation. A lot of what Bergmann does already involves a component of automation, or at least a component of a machine doing work that a human might have otherwise done. In the context of farms, this isn't *quite* as concerning as it might have been when automation first made its way to the supermarket: yes, a lot of farmers depend on farm jobs for their livelihoods – as did (and do) grocery-store clerks – but farming conditions for farm workers can be and are completely abysmal, to the point of being abusive. And this is not sustainable, least of all because a lot of farms depend on migrant workers whose living conditions and earned wages pale in comparison to their passport-holding counterparts: migrant workers in Ontario, for instance, qualify for the Ontario Health Insurance Plan, but that funding expires as soon as their visas do, meaning they can be sent home early. Many pay their own travel costs. Organic or not, the food grown and harvested on many conventional farms in Canada crosses the line into immorality, by any standard of human decency, as far as the working conditions surrounding its growth and harvest are concerned. This is another flaw of the prevailing conversation surrounding food that is good and right: the human element is often ignored.

Still, even if we're replacing unsustainable or unstable labour practices, should we be doing it with robots – even if they're only picking weeds? In October 2017, a Pew Research study found 70 per cent of Americans fear artificial intelligence means job replacement. This concern is not new or novel – in fact, there's a term for when it becomes a reality: *technological unemployment*, which means job loss caused by innovation, was popularized by economist John Maynard Keynes in the 1930s. Dystopic fiction often focuses on automation and sentient robots as cornerstones in the dissolution of society as we know it; humans, after all, can tell the difference between right and wrong, while robots only know waste vs. efficiency.

Automation it already happening on farms: the technology that Bergmann uses, which overlays data and 'learns' from it, is AI. And it *does* replace work that would have otherwise been done by a farmer, which in Bergmann's case frees him up to do plenty of other stuff, grow plenty of other things, and – ahem – spend time on social media (and why not? It's a smart use of technology to get people more engaged with and aware of farming on a day-to-day basis). And farm AI can already do some remarkable stuff: in summer 2017, a team of Cornell researchers built a neural network that used transfer learning to visually identify disease in cassava crops – and, best of all, the program they developed loads onto a smart phone.

When I broached the topic of automation at Fresh City Farms, Hannah Hunter liked the idea of a weed-picking robot – it would save her time, and probably a few backaches. I don't know what kind of software would fuel the little weed-picker, but it would likely involve a component of machine learning: the robot would know how many weeds grow where, when, and at what rate, and could analyze and deliver conclusions and actionable ideas based on that information. Most smart farm equipment does this, too – in fact, the introduction of AI onto the farm actually has its own name: *decision* agriculture.

On the phone, months after Terroir, Bergmann admits he'd been rattled by the gentleman farmer who approached the mic after his declaration of death upon the family farm. Bergmann approached him later and says he wasn't too receptive to conversation – until the farmer's wife joined in and said, 'Hey, Will the farmer, aren't you the guy with the organic CSA?'

Indeed, Will Bergmann *is* an organic farmer and precision advocate (and GMO supporter, for the record). He contains agricultural multitudes.

'[The farmer] started to talk about the fact that there are practices he uses on his farm that come from conventional (non-organic) farming,' Bergmann recalls. 'We basically came to the agreement that, yeah, there are things we can learn from each other. The thing is: none of us are right. We need to work together to figure things out.'

The core tenet of precision agriculture – the doing and growing of more with less – is particularly resonant with me not just because it makes absolute mathematical sense, but because it was how I was raised to understand the ideal interaction with food, whether I knew it or not.

My mother – and her mother's mother – grew up with an innate understanding of how to stretch a buck, so to speak, in the kitchen. They wasted not and wanted not, sure, but they also ate a bunch of stuff that, especially in the eyes of my mother's classroom peers, was otherwise unrecognizable as food, being as this was decades before things like offal and offcuts became trendy: my mom tells stories about being taunted by her classmates for bringing tongue sandwiches to school, and I still retch a little every time I think of the smell of her seared-then-stewed tripe.

I grew up eating a lot of food that was good for me, and delicious, but cheap: my nonna once joked that her children – my mother and aunt – would complain about eating *pasta e fagioli* (a soup of pasta and beans) multiple nights per week: the dish is high in nutrition and low in cost, and can be stretched with the addition of water and cheap starches. But, after repeat doses, the rustic staple loses all of its gustatory appeal, particularly to young children. My mother didn't subject us to the same meals day in and day out, but when she set out on her twice-monthly grocery runs, she did so with a singular purpose: to get as much as she could for as little as possible. On Friday nights she'd pore over grocery-store flyers, identifying which stores were having the best sales, and on what; on Saturday she would drive from one store to another, filling the trunk with two-for-ones and 50-per-cent-offs. She'd sit down on Sunday to input each receipt bottom line into an actual, physical bank book, then spend the week cooking.

We weren't poor. But we could credit both our hearty, healthy – if at times repetitive – meals *and* our healthy financial situation (at least in part) to my mother's innate instinct for stretching the grocery buck. We ate a lot of beans, a lot of pasta, a lot of rice, and a lot of stewed meat – it didn't taste cheap, and we scraped our plates.

I understand why Bergmann, using precision agriculture, wants to do more with less from a financial perspective, and from an environmental perspective: he has a young family, and it saves him money and benefits the planet. But I was surprised to hear Dr. Lauri Wagter-Lesperance, a researcher at the University of Guelph, cite the doing of more with less as a goal of her work – her field being bovine genetics.

Wagter-Lesperance works with Dr. Bonnie Mallard and a team of other researchers and scientists on (among other things) something called high immune responder technology. HIR is 'a patented testing method to identify cattle with inherently superior immunity and disease resistance,' she explains, which 'naturally improves herd health and productivity. It provides benefits to the producer, the farmer, the consumer, and the animal through the reduced use of antibiotics.'

In layman's terms: HIR tech has allowed Mallard and her fellow researchers to selectively breed cattle for specific genetic advantages. They have developed a way to reliably identify cattle that have a genetic predisposition toward fending off diseases, such as bovine mastitis, which has traditionally required farmers to treat their herds with high quantities of antibiotics. HIR technology is licensed to Semex, a retailer of 'high quality bovine genetics' also based in Guelph. And in 2012, Semex launched Immunity+ Sires, a line of cattle optimized with Mallard's HIR technology.

What Bonnie Mallard and her team do isn't precision farming: it's an advanced version of the selective breeding that livestock farmers have been doing since the dawn of agriculture itself. She's just doing it more quickly, efficiently, and reliably, by working in a laboratory rather than a barn. That's the first 'more with less': more high-performing cattle in less time.

The second 'more for less' has to do with antibiotics, one of the biggest bogeymen as far as industrial meat production is concerned. In identifying and breeding specifically for superior immune response, Mallard's team has all but guaranteed that farmers can produce more product with fewer antibiotics and, therefore, less money.

More succinctly: 'This system,' Mallard and fellow University of Guelph professor Kathleen Thompson-Crispi wrote in a 2013 article for *Hoard's Dairyman*, a trade publication aimed at cattle farmers, 'takes advantage of the animal's own intrinsic ability to mount a robust, balanced and beneficial immune response that is not associated with any GMO. The High Immune Response technology is a new genetic tool for breeding cattle with improved disease resistance that you should consider to aid in disease control.'

Speaking of bogeymen, there's some terminology the Mallard team's research uses that is, as far as sustainable food and farming systems have been concerned, *lingua non grata*: 'genetics,' and all its applicable offshoots. As Mallard and Thompson-Crispi underscore, HIR tech does not involve genetic modification. But it is a type of genetic technology – and, as soon as you say the word *genetics* to many champions of so-called good food, temperaments immediately change. I know this from personal experience: every time I have given the elevator pitch for this book, no sooner is the word out of my mouth than receptiveness and interest turns to skepticism and dismissal.

This skepticism is not without merit. Even referring to cows – living, breathing, feeling animals – as an optimized 'line of sires' with a plus sign beside their name is a bit dystopian; it's more comfortable to think of our food as whole and holistic than as trademarked and patented. And besides, the intersection of genetics and food has, heretofore, largely manifested itself as something reputedly and allegedly evil, corporate, planet-threatening, economically disastrous, and – depending on who you ask – potentially life- and planet-shattering: GMOs.

The first time I heard the name Monsanto, I was in my late teens, at the nadir of my self-styled hippie phase: I wore a hemp purse, signed petitions against the development of a Walmart in Guelph's north end (it came anyway, despite my efforts), had stopped eating meat, and wore a nose ring I thought looked incredibly rebellious, even when it was incredibly infected. I learned about Monsanto from my mother, who mentioned to me offhand during a car ride once that the conglomerate was somehow involved in genetically modified organisms, and was also funding research at the University of Guelph's venerable school of agriculture.

I was scandalized. But that immediate feeling of shock and disgust was the beginning and end of my seeking out of information on what Monsanto was, what it had to do with agriculture, and how exactly it was involved with the university. All I felt I needed to know was that agriculture – i.e., food – was pure; that research was noble and altruistic; and that Monsanto, a giant multinational conglomerate, was, by default, very bad.

Of course, I didn't really *know* anything – I was still in my teens, after all. I also didn't think I needed to find anything out: this was nature vs. science, good vs. capitalism. It was clear which side I'd take. My core lack of knowledge, combined with my visceral aversion, put me in the same league as many opponents of GMOs, who view food geneticists as mad scientists keen on destroying us and the planet we live on with profiteering and Frankenfoods. As Dr. Alison Van Eenennaam says, in the 2017 pro-genetics film *Food Evolution*, 'It's much easier to sell fear than science.'

Food Evolution itself is noteworthy: an entirely pro-GMO documentary whose tone is measured and reasonable, using case studies to demonstrate what gene editing has meant, as far as food is concerned, and what it could mean. The film's through line, though, isn't educational: director Scott Kennedy and his team focus heavily and pointedly on anti-GMO sentiment, noting how frequently it depends on bad science, speculation, confirmation bias, and – most significantly – fear: in this case, fear of the unknown.

Some of the data from the anti-GMO camp is striking in its misrepresentation. An interesting point in *Food Evolution* sees anti-GMO activists correlating the use of Roundup Ready crops, which are engineered using a Monsanto-licensed technology, with an increase in diabetes and obesity. Sure. But, of course, we all know correlation isn't causation; and anyway, couldn't that exact same data sample, using the exact same logic, be used to demonstrate that the rise in obesity correlates to the rise in diabetes? That the rise in diabetes correlates to a rise in the use of Roundup Ready? You could just as easily overlay a fourth data set indicating the rise in global population, and apply the same correlative reasoning to use the chart as proof positive that a rise in the use of Roundup Ready has increased the number of people on earth.

Anti-GMO sentiment, in some ways, mirrors another uniquely twenty-first-century controversy that pits the natural world against the scientific one: the debate over the safeness of vaccines. Anti-vaxxers, as they're known, rely on specious and often dangerously false pillars to make their point, the most notable of which is a study by Andrew Wakefield that suggested a link between measles vaccines and autism. The study was discredited in 1998, and Wakefield was stripped of his medical licence not long after. Nevertheless, his work – and his so-called findings – catapulted anti-vaccine sentiment into the limelight, championed by Hollywood A-listers and mommy bloggers alike, all using the same false logic and junk science.

Anti-GMO activists have their own version of the Wakefield study: a 2012 paper authored by French researchers led by Gilles-Éric Séralini that claimed to demonstrate that lab rats that were fed Monsanto-developed GM corn developed cancerous tumours and died more quickly than a control group of rats. The study, originally published in the journal *Food and Chemical Toxicology*, was retracted by the journal in 2013 after a firestorm from the scientific community over the study's supposed inadequate statistical refereeing – but it was republished in 2014 by the journal *Environmental Sciences Europe*, to give the scientific community guaranteed long-term access to its data.

In fairness to genetics skeptics, genetically engineered food crops might pose health risks. But they might not — currently, there's no compelling evidence to prove that they do and, as TV host John Oliver noted in his *Last Week Tonight* segment on vaccination, 'proving a negative is an impossible standard': it's much easier to argue that something is not good than to prove that it's not *not* good.

And that's where it gets complicated, as if it wasn't complicated already. There are plenty of reasons to distrust Monsanto in particular and genetic modification of food crops in general, because the initial public rollout of GM products was — to put it euphemistically but succinctly — not great. If genetic engineering of food crops was now and forever limited to the GMOs and associated practices that have the most public awareness — such as Roundup Ready crops and barring farmers from seed-saving — then it's not unfair to suggest we ought to put a halt to the whole thing.

But, of course, that's not all there is to it.

In October 2017, the podcast *This American Life* aired an episode called 'Things I Mean to Know.' In its intro, journalist Diane Wu remembers attending a talk, in a small town in Germany, by Harry Kroto, a Nobel-winning chemist. At one point, she remembers, Kroto halted his train of thought suddenly and asked members of the audience: 'How many of you believe the sun revolves around the earth?' Being the type of crowd who would show up to hear a Nobel-winning chemist talk, there were chuckles, and no hands were raised. Then Kroto asked the opposite:

'How many of you believe the earth revolves around the sun?' An auditorium's worth of hands shot into the air, without a second thought.

And then, Wu recalls, Kroto asked something that shook her so hard, she couldn't pay attention to the rest of the lecture: 'How many of you know the evidence for that? How many of you know the evidence that the earth revolves around the sun?'

Very few hands were raised. And Kroto was disappointed. 'He kind of chided us,' she says, that they'd taken it 'on faith. "How much else have you accepted without evidence? Because that is one of the most serious problems facing our civilization today."'

With all due respect to Kroto, it might be a problem, but for those of us who aren't members of the scientific community, there is always going to be a modicum of taking scientists at their word; even now, having – like Wu – looked up the evidence for the earth revolving around the sun, it would be difficult, if not impossible, for me to explain that evidence to another person. Science isn't easy, and there is a strong onus on the general populace to take much of it on faith. We should, anyway. A lot of it is pretty amazing.

The word *faith* is difficult, though, because technically it doesn't belong in conversations having to do with empirical data and demonstrable facts and findings. We don't *have* *faith* in science; we know it. People like to quote and requote and requote again Neil deGrasse Tyson on this one. 'The good thing about science,' he said in a panel discussion on the HBO show *Real Time*, 'is that it's true whether or not you believe in it.' This is also where the conversation surrounding the viability of genetically modified organisms takes a sharp left turn into moralistic territory: we will take things on faith that adhere to our pre-existing views about the world and our place in it, and disregard things as false and wrong that oppose those views – often without having the whole picture. An environmental activist who believes in the science that backs climate change – even without being able to explain or quantify the exact mechanisms and risks of climate change – might be more likely to take on faith the assertion that GMOs are bad, though this is kind of contradictory: there's plenty of scientific evidence for the former and plenty of bunk science in support of the latter. Conversely, an anti-vaxxer with a strong distrust of main-stream scientific research might be just as opposed to GMOs, basing that distrust on a completely different confirmation bias than that of the aforementioned environmental activist.

It becomes difficult to know who *should* believe in genetic intervention into our food and agriculture systems, based on what they already believe. If the pro-science people aren't necessarily on board, and neither are the anti-science conspiracy theorists, then genetic engineering activists have an extremely tough sell on their hands: how do you sell science to everyone when it's seemingly attractive to no one?

In 2009, the *Guardian* ran a series of essays from contributors who purported to answer the question 'Should we believe in belief?' It's a particularly interesting read from the perspective of the Trump era; it seems almost quaint in its headiness and enthusiastic tackling of such esotericism. Since the election of 2016, what we believe to be true has taken on a galling new shape, as the forty-fifth US president has waged an active, consistent war on the scientific and journalistic communities.

So, when it comes to GMOs, it's difficult to know what to believe, when, and how much. As a member of the non-scientific community, I accept that I have taken on faith the assertions of the pro-genetics camp. For lack of the ability to verify their claims against my own knowledge rather than against my sentimental preference for scientific innovation over conspiracy, I have no choice but to trust them.

The primary trouble with the distrust in GMOs is that consumer suspicion of potentially *harmful* GMOs has prevented the implementation of potentially *helpful* genetic editing; the well is effectively poisoned. There is so much fear-mongering, so much mistrust, that it's near impossible to get this research out of the lab and into the world. Progress on genetics as it pertains to food – big progress, scary progress, potentially life-changing progress – has more or less halted. 'The amount of skepticism and misinformation has greatly held back technology that exists, and that's been demonstrated as being effective,' says Kevin Folta, chair of the horticultural sciences department at the University of Florida. 'It's a movement that has a body count.'

On that last point, Folta – who I spoke to while he was on his way to Uganda to attend a conference on biotechnology and food security – means there are advancements in the gene editing of food crops that could potentially benefit developing countries, and keep alive people who might otherwise die due to a lack of access to food. One case study in *Food Revolution* focuses on bananas in Uganda, which are widely affected by a disease called banana wilt. Scientists have found that the insertion of a gene from sweet pepper plants makes these bananas resistant to the disease, but bananas that have been engineered with the pepper gene so far exist only in a research capacity.

And it's hard to know how to move forward, though Folta, the makers of *Food Evolution*, and other pro-science pundits have some suggestions. For one, Folta says, use the right words: GMO, he argues, is an unscientific term – *genetic engineering* is more correct. 'Genetic modification is what happens upon a sexual crossing, mutation, multiplication of chromosomes, introduction of a single new gene from an unrelated species, or the tweaking of a genome with new gene-editing techniques,' he wrote in a *Medium* piece in 2017. 'These are all examples of genetic modification, but not all offer the predictability and precision of the process of genetic engineering.' He also emphasizes that there's not really such a thing as 'genetically engineered foods' – engineered food *crops*, yes, and that's a fundamentally different thing.

It could also help if people knew precisely what gene editing is: the creation of an organism that has had its DNA altered by the insertion of a gene that's outside its genetic makeup. Or that we already depend on things that are technically classified as genetically modified organisms, like insulin. Perhaps it would be useful to emphasize that a slower form of genetic engineering – selective breeding – has been used by farmers for centuries.

Rebranding is a great idea, but using different terminology doesn't take away from the mistrust. 'It freaks people out,' says Evan Fraser, 'but I'm going to say the public debate is fifteen years behind the science.'

There is an extreme misanthropy that accompanies the denial of innovation as a move forward. Humans have changed the earth and, as Folta says, have changed the plants as we grew them, but anti-conventional agriculture activists will now position human innovation as the opposite of progress. The same can be said of the public debate around genetically engineered food crops: why would we use innovation to solve our food problems, when innovation is what got us here in the first place? Shouldn't we just turn everything back to the land, admit we screwed up, and let nature take its course?

It's another example of the polarized thinking that complicates our contemporary idea of what constitutes sustainable food and sustainable food systems. And here, as elsewhere, it's a hugely ideological, emotionally charged debate. Anti-GMO activists don't just rally against genetic intervention, they evangelize against it, using cases that prey on our emotional instincts rather than our common sense. Many question how we can justify feeding these foods to our children, for instance, suggesting those who are onside with genetic engineering are, somehow, guilty of bad parenting – that if we do not eat organic, do not disavow corporate involvement in the food chain, do not have the desire and means and ability to eat organic food 100 per cent of the time, we are fundamentally, morally bad.

If you ask Folta – someone who has accepted large sums of money from Monsanto for his research (much to his detriment, after a clumsy *New York Times* story in 2016 painted him as little more than a corporate shill) – we ought to distrust, if not Monsanto in particular, then corporations at large when they meddle with our food supply. Fraser thinks so, too: 'Who benefits from this technology?' he wonders. 'When you move into the developing world, I think there's a serious critique to be had.' But distrust of corporate interest isn't a case against genetic engineering – though, considering how many researchers, scientists, and post-secondary institutions rely on such private funding, it would be irresponsible to suggest we shouldn't always ask who's paying for what, and why.

And anyway, as the planet warms, we are facing serious risks to our food crops – risks that are exacerbated in non-Western countries – and food researchers are taking these risks into account. Drought resistance is among the key traits that genetically engineered foods are optimized to have; Folta notes that one of his colleagues is working on a type of corn that contains 35 per cent more protein when grown at hotter temperatures. Back in Bonnie Mallard's lab, members of the team are looking at applying HIR technology to dairy cows, which traditionally underperform in warmer temperatures. The team hopes to apply HIR methods to identify cows that still perform – still produce adequate milk – when it gets hot, in order to develop a line of what Fraser calls 'climate-change-resistant dairy cows.'

It seems like solving the wrong problem – making sure we'll still have cheese when the planet warms rather than stopping the planet from warming – but it's also pragmatic: if we can't make everyone stop eating animal proteins, and we can't cool the planet, we might as well work with what we've got and solve for the best possible outcome.

There aren't a lot of genetically modified foodstuffs on the market in North America. In Canada, there is, notably, genetically modified salmon produced by the company AquaBounty; it's engineered to grow twice as fast as regular salmon, was approved for sale in 2016, and, as of summer 2017, more than 4.5 tonnes of the stuff had already been consumed by Canadians (to, at the time of writing, no ill effect). It's the first genetically engineered animal approved for sale in Canada.

In British Columbia, a company called Okanagan Specialty Fruits has – since November 2017 – been selling genetically modified apples that it grows south of the border, to residents of the United States. The Arctic Apple is a trademarked breed whose genetic modification prevents it from browning when cut; this allows Okanagan Specialty Fruits to sell Arctic Apples as precut slices. On the surface, this seems like an odd, trivial, aesthetic-only use of a complicated technology: who truly cares if an apple browns? Why sell a precut apple slice, anyway? Can't we just bite into apples anymore?

These were my thoughts, at least. I like climate-change-resistant dairy cows because I want to have brie at the end of the world and I'm interested in engineering food crops for drought and disease resistance because I'm afraid of how much food will be wiped out by increasingly erratic and unpredictable weather patterns. But a precut apple that doesn't brown? This is where my own sense of moral superiority rears its head: are we really so lazy?

Okanagan's owner, orchardist and bioresource engineer Neal Carter, puts it in perspective for me. 'We looked at the price returns we were getting for apples, and the fact that apple consumption is declining,' he says (the 'we' is him and his wife, Louisa, OSF's other founder). 'If you're a tree-fruit grower, it's not good news when your customer is choosing an alternative. At the same time, the fresh-cut-produce industry is taking off. We looked at the carrot, the baby-carrot-type concept, and how it was driving carrot consumption, and carrot consumption doubled between 1988 and 1995. We thought, wow, if we could cut apples into slices and make them available in a bag, we could guide buyers' decisions.'

The science behind the Arctic Apple is called 'PPO silencing.' Primary browning – the aesthetic discolouration you see taking place on apples left to sit uneaten on fruit trays and in fruit salads – is a type of oxidization that's driven by the enzyme polyphenol oxidase (PPO). To effectively silence this enzyme, OSF inserts a 'low PPO-producing gene sequence – dubbed GEN-03 – …into the parent cultivar's DNA.' The Arctic Apple, as a result, produces significantly fewer PPOs than conventional apples, and it doesn't go brown.

In 2015, shortly after OSF received regulatory appeal to begin retailing the Arctic Apple (which currently grows in Washington State), the company was bought by Intrexon, a US-based synthetic biology company (their website is, ominously, dna.com). At the time, Carter says, 'with the increasing amount of anti-GM headwinds, the companies that wanted to take that non-browning apple were less enthusiastic to be first. We had a lineup of people who wanted to be second.

'When we started in 1997, in North America, there really wasn't much in the way of anti-GM movement,' he continues. 'It wasn't until 1999, 2000, that we saw it picking up. We see it as another tool in the toolbox, for plant breeding. From my own perspective, using the best tool in the toolbox is how you want to do things. Using the apple's own genes seems like such an innocuous use of the technology, and I believe it differentiates us from other products, like Roundup Ready soybeans or Bt corn [a GMO crop developed to resist pests]. We believe that it's the right technology, and we believe that the product speaks for itself.'

Whether consumers will believe that remains to be seen, of course. But Carter makes a few compelling points about the use of genetic technology here that, initially, I had not considered: gene silencing allows the Arctic Apple to forego the use of chemicals that are otherwise present on products in what Carter terms the 'sliced-apple category.' And when apples brown – even when it's only the type of browning that's mainly aesthetic – people don't want to eat them; apples that don't brown, it therefore stands to reason, are less likely to go to waste.

This is all, admittedly, a significant dumbing-down of OSF's processes, goals, and marketing approaches. Luckily for anyone interested, the company is almost disconcertingly transparent about its techniques, methodologies, processes, and goals on its website; the aim seems to be to demystify genetic modification first, which will in turn lead to the most important thing any farmers working with genetic processes will require of the general public: trust, leading to the ability to accept things on faith.

A few weeks before Christmas last year, I went out for dinner with a friend to celebrate his recent purchase of a house in my neighbourhood. I'd just gotten over the flu, so I wasn't feeling hungry, and I conceded to his choice of venue: a narrow bar called the Hole in the Wall that guaranteed decent beer for me and, for him, a palatable veggie burger.

Western consumers love meat, and we eat it at alarming rates: Canadians gobble up around 23.4 kilograms of meat per person per year, which seems like a lot, but pales in comparison to the meat-consumption habits of our neighbours to the south, where the amount is almost double that. Meat consumption is hugely taxing, economically and environmentally: according to NPR's *The Salt*, in order to produce a quarter of a pound of beef, it takes 6.8 pounds of grain (for feed), 52.8 gallons of water (for drinking and crop irrigation), 74.5 square feet of land (for feed crops and grazing cattle), and 1,036 Btus of fossil-fuel-based energy. Multiply each of those figures by 23.4 – or by 46 – and it might begin to seem like cutting meat from our diets completely would solve many, if not all, of the problems plaguing our current food systems: we'd have more land for fruits and vegetables, more water for, well, everything, and would end up cutting back on the use of fossil fuels on an astronomical level.

This is not necessarily the most productive approach. By all accounts, our global overconsumption of meat is a problem – but the idea of complete and total abstinence is far from being the solution. In fact, a group of researchers performed a study that aimed to measure what, theoretically, would happen if residents of the US stopped eating meat; they published their findings in September 2017, in the journal *Proceedings of the National Academy of Sciences of the United States of America* (PNAS). Plants-only agriculture, the researchers said, would result in a net elimination of greenhouse gases, but while the system 'produced 23% more food, it met fewer of the US population's requirements for essential nutrients. When nutritional adequacy was evaluated by using least-cost diets produced from foods available, more nutrient deficiencies, a greater excess of energy, and a need to consume a greater amount of food solids were encountered in plants-only diets.' In other words, if you get rid of meat, we all have to purchase, prepare, and eat more food overall. 'Getting rid of animal agriculture would,' the report concludes, 'create a food supply incapable of supporting the US population's nutritional requirements.'

This is not a new idea: advocates in Canada's northernmost provinces have bemoaned the idea of container farming and greenhouses as total solutions to food insecurity in those locations, since survival in cold climates requires a greater caloric input, and meat is extremely calorie-dense (also, its harvest and consumption is culturally important to the Indigenous populations that live in the northern hemisphere). Frankly, considering the human impact of plant-based eating over the health of animals and the planet is often the missing part of the let's-all-go-vegan conversation: the same PNAS report notes that, in the US alone, animal agriculture employs '1.6×10^6 people and accounts for \$31.8 billion in exports.' That's 1.6 million people whose jobs would disappear. And while the model put forth by the PNAS researchers is, to put it lightly, extreme – whether we want it to or not, no industry will simply cease to exist overnight – it pours a very cold bucket of water on the idea that the elimination of animal food products is the path toward sustainability.

What we really should do, obviously, is eat way, way, way less meat – maybe go vegan before 6:00 p.m., like Mark Bittman, or tuck into a cut of flesh only in restaurants (and even then, only the good ones). There's still a nutritional void created here. When I was a teenaged vegetarian, lentils, chickpeas, and tofu simply didn't cut it; I would slather whole-wheat bread with mayonnaise and stack it with vegan 'turkey'; I'd scramble 'ground round' into my eggs; I'd order veggie burgers at fast-food restaurants; and in all of these instances, I'd feel a vast moral (and perhaps also physical) superiority to my peers simply because I was eating food that wasn't meat, which made it, by default, better.

Meat substitutes are conceptually super-weird, particularly when you consider that many vegetarians and vegans forego the consumption of animal products for ethical reasons: why would you want to replicate the experience of eating flesh if you have such strong moral reservations against doing so? Nutritionally, and in terms of calorie input, though, it begins to make a bit more sense, particularly in the North American context, where we seem to have forgotten to build a meal around anything but animal protein. But since these substitutes are deeply processed – and made from soy, one of the most pervasively problematic commodity crops in North America – is substituting meat with meat substitutes really any more good?

I think it depends on how it's done, Take the Silicon Valley–developed Impossible Burger, a plant-based vegetable whose main selling point seems to be the fact that it bleeds – just like real meat! Now, I don't think most vegetarians necessarily want this, a plant that bleeds, but it's appealing to meat-eaters looking to cut down on consumption because it promises a tactile experience that's exactly like the real thing, but without the 6.8 pounds of grain, 52.8 gallons of water, 74.5 square feet of land, 1,036 Btus of fossil-fuel-based energy, and all the attendant guilt.

The thing is: it's not great. Or so I hear. My recent-homeowner vegetarian friend has tried the Impossible Burger and, over a starchier veggie burger at a pub in Toronto's west end, he assured me that it's 'good – not great.' In *New York Magazine*'s recent vegan-food encyclopedia, that opinion is echoed: 'it...has a mushy mouthfeel, a slightly unpleasant aftertaste, and lacks the heft and complex flavour of real beef. Close but no cigar about sums it up.'

Impossible Burger aside – because, by all accounts, it ought to be set aside – there is something of a revolution underway in terms of how we eat meat-free. So much so that 'plant-based' restaurants are de rigueur: places where non-meat-eaters and carnivores alike can enjoy dining experiences that are decadent, thoughtful, and elevated in a culinary sense without sacrificing a single animal in the process. They're good places to eat, in other words, not just vegan places.

And if we can't bring ourselves to eat smoked carrots that are pretending to be hot dogs, as is the case at Toronto's Planta, we might at least find ourselves morally amenable to eating meat without the *footprint* of meat. Lab-grown meat, or cultured meat, has recently been touted as a solution to the fact that we just can't suppress our carnivorous urges – but this one requires getting over a whole new psychological hurdle, and it's a real toughie: if we are skeptical of food whose ingredients we can't pronounce, eating flesh grown in a petri dish seems leaps and bounds away from cognitive acceptance. But we might need to get there: in a 2011 study cited by a *Washington Post* article on lab-grown meat 'calculated that growing meat in labs would cut down on the land required to produce steaks, sausages and bacon by 99% and reduce the associated need for water by 90%.' Not to mention the fact that growing meat in a sterile lab would reduce – if not eliminate – the need for antibiotic intervention in our animal proteins.

The processing required to grow a burger in a lab isn't the same as the kind that gets cheese flavour into tortilla chips. But it nevertheless takes what's on our plate a step (or two, or three) away from the accepted idea that a sustainable food product is a food product whose farmer we know, whose provenance we are familiar with, and whose field, barn, or orchard we could visit and walk away from without fearing for the future of our planet and its inhabitants. Under these tenets – and the tenets that a morally, ethically good food is a whole food, and that anything else is bad – the scientific tampering-with of meat is easy to categorize as an unnatural, Willy Wonka–reminiscent abomination.

Plus the idea of lab-grown meat as panacea for our meat-based woes is largely theoretical, since the stuff is too expensive to produce to actually be anywhere near the consumer market: as of August 2013, a single lab-grown burger costs US$330,000. In the *Atlantic* in 2013, writer Alexis Madrigal estimated that we won't see commercially produced lab-grown meat until 2035. Will we still care by then? (Will we still be around?) And then there's the question of intellectual property: who owns the process it takes to grow cultured meat, and what are the implications of this ownership to consumers who want to shop ethically but can't afford the high prices of a patented process?

As *Gizmodo* science writer Ryan F. Mandelbaum said in his August 2017 article 'Behind the Hype of "Lab-Grown Meat,' the potential future importance of petri-dish pork chops might be a bit overblown:

> [O]verly positive press and ethical optimism can make us dream of a world that doesn't yet exist, where all meat is brewed in a bioreactor, instead of a future where we pursue other options that solve the problems of industrial agriculture. It's exciting that a version of the future feels like it's around the corner, but folks have been writing about lab-grown meat since at least 2003, without a commercial product to show

for it. It doesn't exist yet, at least not in a way that you, a consumer, can eat it.

Which is not to say that – as one expert quoted in Mandelbaum's piece suggests – lab-grown meat is not *a* future of meat; it's just not *the* future of meat. 'I think the way food and technology will mix will be much more complicated than any one current vision might offer,' Christina Agapakis, biologist and creative director of Ginkgo Bioworks, said. The first hurdle might be scaling lab-grown meat outfits up into something commercially viable; but the next step, if the next step comes, will be convincing people this stuff is safe, sustainable, and – if this proves to be the case – important. Considering our track record when it comes to GMOs, one wonders if this future will ever come to pass.

This is all a lot to take in, and a lot of new ideas to put into practice. For hundreds of years, humanity has farmed, grown, raised, and harvested food in largely the same way – even industrial processes, damaging as they have been, have followed a more or less straightforward approach to agriculture, albeit one that is scaled up and watered down past the point of sustainability. And as many have lost faith in the idea of industrial, mechanized food-production processes involving a high level of human intervention, we have defaulted to our age-old belief that doing things the old-fashioned way is the *only* way – as if moving past our current mistakes requires turning back the clock to a way of living that we can empirically demonstrate was more good.

Of course, demonstrating the goodness of the processes of the past in a way that suggests they'll work for the present requires actively ignoring a lot of our current realities – not least among them the fact that old-school agrarian processes worked only because we had fewer people to feed. And we had more time to spend on food, as well: tied into the idea that slow food is good food is the notion that fast food – which could mean food that is made, eaten, or grown more quickly than it ought to be – is lazy food, ignorant food, bad food. Unless we're mimicking the habits of our fore-bears, in other words, we're transgressing.

It's odd that this type of morality is still widely accept-able in the food sphere, because it doesn't really pass muster anywhere else – or, at least, in any circles that consider their thinking progressive and altruistic. It's difficult for people to undo long-held beliefs, to compromise morality, to accept new processes and truths as being more fair, just, and correct than the ones we've simply taken on faith. Where morality is concerned, progress is slow, because it takes a long time to debunk irrationality with facts – dogma simply doesn't respond to the truth. But the overarching truth here is that food doesn't grow on faith – it's always been a scientific process, and it's long been a process dependent on our intervention. As the planet approaches a population of nine billion, those fishes and loaves aren't going to divide themselves.

4

Harvesting Silicon Valley

One Tuesday evening, I decided to build a Personal Food Computer.

Or, I guess, I decided to see what would go into building a food computer, if I had the time, means, and skills, using the Massachusetts Institute of Technology's OpenAg project. OpenAg is an open-source initiative that harnesses a lot of existing tech and coding methodologies and resources to help people all over the world build, manage, and troubleshoot their own indoor food-growing...modules, let's call them. To further simplify, it's a computer programmer's version of hobby farming. OpenAg sounds nerdy, and it is: MIT's medium-scale food computer is a 'Food Server'; its theoretical industrial-scale model is a 'Food Data Center' – but it's also an example of how information technology can throw its hat into the ring concerning the future of sustainable food systems. To wit: OpenAg's ethos is that 'the precursor to a healthier and more sustainable food system will be the creation of an open-source ecosystem of technologies that enable and promote transparency, networked experimentation, education, and hyper-local production.'

The first thing you see on the OpenAg website is a schematic for what, exactly, a food computer looks like. To the layperson – i.e., me – it looks just like a regular computer, but with plants in it. And that's sort of what it is: MIT defines the Personal Food Computer as a 'tabletop-sized, controlled environment agriculture technology platform.' You might call it a tiny, personal-sized vertical farm – like an Easy-Bake Oven, but for basil.

Even without my own dedicated, open-source computer for food, tech has fundamentally altered the way I – and millions of others – eat. For those of us who live in urban centres, just about anything you could ever want to eat is available for purchase (and delivery) at just about any time, with just a few swipes of a smart phone. If industrial agriculture placed a psychological rift between what's on our plates and how it gets there, food- and grocery-delivery apps double down, replacing thoughtfulness and planning with speed and convenience – more than ever before – at mealtime.

And as the food industry capitalizes on the sharing economy – successfully, it should be noted: according to a *New York Times* report, the number of UberEats deliveries multiplied by twenty-four from March 2016 to March 2017 – an opportunity has arisen for advocates of sustainability to do the same. 'There's a growing realization,' says Donna Ratchford, director of the Culture and Strategic Policy Branch for the Culture Division of Ontario's Ministry of Tourism, Culture and Sport, 'that the road to really solving these problems is partnerships and innovations and disruptions and new ways of looking at problems with new problem-solvers.'

I spoke to Ratchford a few days after she helped put on the ShareON Design Jam at Ryerson University. The annual event challenges participants to use technology to implement and influence social change. Each year, the challenge centres on a topic; in 2017, that was food waste and food insecurity. The winning team's idea: Eatonomy, an app that connects users with soon-to-expire food in their neighbourhoods. Eatonomy wraps food insecurity and food waste in one tidy package, though. 'Our mission,' its Facebook page reads, 'is to make good food more affordable for everyone, and to reduce the amount of food wasted in Canada.'

(Eatonomy is only halfway there: as food writer Corey Mintz noted in an article about ShareON, many of those who deal with issues of food insecurity 'are poor, often homeless, and suffer from mental illness and/or drug addiction, and services to help them are underfunded. Gamifying an app will not address their food insecurity.')

But it might address waste – and waste is a huge problem. In Canada, an estimated $31 billion in food is wasted each year, much of it lost at the consumer level. Evan Fraser opines that, 'if food was more expensive, we'd store it better,' but then 'you'd have to swap food waste for food security.' It's a frustrating paradox – that people who live in the developed world waste an estimated one hundred kilograms of food per person, yet there are those for whom good food is an unattainable luxury – but the pieces don't fit together quite so: in our conversation, Ratchford was clear that the Design Jam's themes, waste and food insecurity, were meant to be thought of as separate, echoing the sentiment pervasive among many food-insecurity advocacy organizations that food destined for a wealthy person's garbage should not be considered the solution to the impoverished person's hunger. The system needs to be rejigged so that no one is even hypothetically expected to live on someone else's kitchen scraps. The conflation of these issues – and the difficulty in accepting them full-stop as separate problems to be solved separately – is indicative of an approach that's endemic to the conversations that exist within the sustainable-food sphere: trying to solve for all problems, all at once. The problems facing food production and food systems are so varied, their implications so wide-reaching, and their destructive nature so urgent that this approach is completely understandable. But it has resulted in a selection of supposedly catch-all solutions (Eat local! Eat organic! Cook at home!) that, while attractive in their curative claims, are impractical (if not ineffective) in their application. But when there's only one cure being offered, you'll take it – even if it's a bit of snake oil.

When Ratchford explains the Design Jam, she says that the challenge posed to participants each year is to solve for problems using 'design thinking' – and, according to MIT, 'The first step in design thinking is to understand the problem you are trying to solve before searching for solutions.' For Eatonomy, the problem is limited to food waste – it's not really practical for addressing food waste *and* food insecurity. If you look at it like that, it's a great idea (so great it already exists in the real world as Flashfood, an app that partners with grocery stores to offer deeply discounted, almost-expired food, and with farms to offer similarly inexpensive produce deemed too ugly for conventional retail).

It wasn't the first time in recent months that the idea of design-as-sustainability-panacea had crossed my path. In October 2017, I visited the annual Expo for Design, Innovation and Technology in Toronto. EDITX is a sort of art-exhibition-meets-think-tank-meets-symposium-meets-museum, where a group of multi-hyphenates posit design-focused solutions to the problems of the future. At the 2017 exhibition, these were – for lack of a better word – problems that skewed toward the functionally human. I wasn't surprised, then, to find that a huge amount of real estate in the former Unilever factory that housed EDITX was dedicated to suggesting design-, tech-, and innovation-focused approaches to the future of food. A lot of these were, at this point, the sorts of things I'd come to expect: indoor farming (aquaponics, hydroponics), alternative proteins (bugs), and zero-footprint food-production prototypes (a closed-loop system that turns the by-products of craft-beer production into animal feed).

But there were also a lot of what MIT might call Food Computers: businesses selling teeny-tiny personal farming systems, boasting the life- and planet-saving benefits of homegrown greens and herbs (without the need to code or program anything).

For as long as people have been confined to small, indoor living spaces, we've thought about ways to grow our own food inside. Recently, for instance, I was able to keep a small rosemary plant alive in my living room for a personal-record-setting three months (I'm not great at plant care). Others have had more luck: I can't count the number of apartments and condos I've visited with windows lined with beautiful, fresh herbs. But as more of us are forced into less space – and space that's farther above ground, literally farther from the soil – and, as a by-product of density, as space itself continues to disappear in favour of human development, there's an increasing urgency, coupled with attractiveness, to the idea of putting tiny little farms into our tiny little apartments.

This is a step removed from how we've traditionally come to think of vertical farming, which is in the same vein as we have come to think of food production as a whole: something that someone else – or something else, like a company or corporation – is responsible for. Food Computers and the like are a uniquely individualized way of putting food-procurement agency back into the hands of consumers, if only on a teeny-tiny, lettuce-and-herbs-scale. The distance from farm to table could be only a few feet, if we allow our definition of 'farm' to include something that MIT calls a computer.

Silicon Valley, of course, is already on it. In an April 2017 feature in the *Ringer*, Alyssa Bereznak examined the myriad ways the tech industry is looking to capitalize on the idea of urban farming. 'The history of urban farming in the United States has always been inextricably linked to the availability of food, and a community's ability to grow that food itself,' Bereznak wrote. And the way the community – any community, but particularly an urban community – has been able to grow food has fundamentally changed; largely, urban communities don't grow their own food. In the *Ringer* piece, a company called Bowery, a vertical-farming outfit located in New Jersey, positions itself as the next logical step of the organic movement: according to CEO Irving Fain, who is interviewed extensively for the piece, 'A lot of what the organic movement was about was how do we create a farming practice that allows better or slower regeneration and better protection of the land around us while also growing a higher quality food product. And that was a great step. When the organic standards were written, a lot of the technology that we use today didn't even exist. What we're able to do at Bowery is the next evolution, the next step, from what organic was able to do from where industrial agriculture was before.'

Bowery is a farm, by unconventional standards. But more than that, it's a start-up, using proprietary software – which Fain charmingly (if a bit Orwellianly) calls FarmOS – to grow produce. It has raised more than $7 million in venture funds. And Bowery isn't alone in the farm-to-tech sphere: back at EDITX, a large section of the Bruce Mau–curated main exhibit, called *Prosperity for All*, was dedicated to the work of venture capitalist-turned-restaurateur Kimbal Musk (yes, he's Elon's brother), a vertical-farming advocate who has gone on record saying that 'food is the new internet.'

One of Musk's initiatives is Square Roots, an urban farming accelerator that gives aspiring growers the opportunity to flex their farming muscles in shipping containers, where they test and develop their own individual urban- and vertical-farming models. He's also behind Learning Gardens, four hundred edible schoolyards scattered across the US. But despite these seemingly noble – and sort of innocuous – efforts, Musk is a controversial figure. In September 2017, writer and *Edible Manhattan* editor Brian Halweil tweeted a quotation from Musk, who was speaking at a Food Tank Summit: 'Food is one of the final frontiers that technology hasn't tackled yet. If we do it well, it will mean good food for all.'

It made people angry – partially because, as Halweil later pointed out in an *Edible Manhattan* piece, the quotation was taken partially out of context. But it's also because farmers *do* use technology. So Musk clarified, and Halweil reported the clarification:

> In Musk's reply, he made an important distinction between harnessing all the innovation not just to produce mountains of food – something our industrial food system is very good at – but producing 'real food' that is accessible to all people. 'Sorry. Misquoted/mis-spoke. We've applied technology to ag for thousands of years. Modern technology is only now working on #realfood.

Which, really, is the crux of the whole thing: in as yet undefined ways, for an as yet undefined segment of the population, in ways that are as yet determined to be more or less sustainable, technology has – according to a Musk brother, at least – the potential to revolutionize the quality of food to which all people have access, while utilizing drastically fewer environmental and human resources. That's why, in the clarification above, Musk makes a point of noting that modern technology has now set its sights on the revolutionizing of so-called 'real food.' In the past, the intersection of modern science and food systems has resulted in hyperprocessed, mass-produced facsimiles of food (McDonald's, for instance, or TV dinners), whose primary aim was convenience; twenty-first-century food technology might be all about how to build a better (and faster-growing, more nutritious, more affordable) tomato. A *real* tomato. Because while it is factually accurate that the current global food system produces enough *calories* to feed everyone on earth, we aren't producing enough healthful food, the five to ten servings of fruit or vegetables per day recommended by Canada's Food Guide and others.

It's a necessary shift, and a frightening one: what does tech-produced food look like? Taste like? At what point do FarmOS and AI eliminate more farming jobs than they create? And if computer technology is the future of farming, do those with limited technological aptitudes – and/or those too deeply entrenched in systemic food insecurity to appreciate gamified apps – get shut out?

Maybe those aren't the right questions – particularly because, like every other tech-driven approach to feeding the planet into the future, the Silicon Valley model – startups, venture capital, and disruption – isn't a cure-all: it's just part of a bigger picture. And anyway, Silicon Valley doesn't have it all figured out either. As Bereznak writes, the 'true question of Silicon Valley investors is almost always: Can a business scale up? Is it a Foursquare (doomed to mild popularity) or an Uber (able to expand at a near-terrifying pace)? The question is particularly tricky for something as intricately designed and finicky as a farm, which can't simply be revamped by overhauling a portion of code or redesigning its user experience.'

When I was a kid, I was really into paleontology; I never saw *Jurassic Park*, but I knew the Jurassic *period* was a point in the planet's history defined not only by the tectonic location of earth's landmasses, but also by the creatures that inhabited those landmasses (though, if you asked me now which dinosaurs were alive during the period, I'd probably only be able to accurately identify the *Tyrannosaurus rex* – because of the movie, not the books I read in elementary school). As anyone who's been to the prehistoric wing of any museum can tell you, the planet has been through a number of geologic periods; the one we're currently in has been – unofficially, it bears noting – termed the Anthropocene, for its human influence. In her 2010 book *The Human Age: The World Shaped by Us*, Diane Ackerman investigates not only how we have changed the planet, but how we continue to evolve as a reflection of those changes. Technology, of course, plays no small part; the book's introductory chapter is, tellingly, called 'Apps for Apes.'

'Our inventions,' she writes, 'don't just change our minds; they modify our gray and white matter, rewiring the brain and priming it for a different mode of living, problem-solving, and adapting. In the process, a tapestry of new thoughts arises, and one's worldview changes.' Humanity has undergone this type of mental transformation time and time again as we've evolved alongside the things we've created; this sort of rewiring, rethinking, and changing of behaviour can certainly be applied to our respective and collective relationship with food. Food was originally given the industrialized, processed treatment to respond to a growing need for speed and convenience; in turn, our attitudes evolved to *expect* speed and convenience, and the food industry responded and evolved further. That need for speed and convenience has now extended to – and matched up with – our relationship to technology: we want everything better, faster, and more instantaneously in line with what we need at any given moment – and we can have it, thanks to an army of developers, marketers, innovators, and disrupters keen to capitalize on our growing technological dependence, and the fact that we'll always need to eat.

I don't think Silicon Valley or its attendant mindsets and philosophies are fundamentally good – no more than I think organic food, farmers' markets, or GMOs are fundamentally good. But the idea of the start-up-focused, tech-minded school of thinking that has profoundly altered human thought and behaviour over the past decade working on the issue of food and sustainable food production is remarkably affecting. When I think about the future of food, I put it in the context of who we are now, as a species; and when I think about that, a line from an October 2017 *New York Magazine* article about Facebook comes to mind: '"monthly active Facebook users" is the single largest non-biologically sorted group of people on the planet after "Christians" – and, growing consistently at around 17% year after year, it could surpass that group before the end of 2017 and encompass one-third of the world's population by this time next year.' The easiest way to reach a whole bunch of people at once is digitally. It's been like that for a long time.

Back in Toronto, some disrupters are already doing just that. Feedback is a Toronto-based app that partners with restaurants to sell surplus at a discount. Both Feedback and the aforementioned Eatonomy benefit businesses and the environment. And in the case of Feedback, there's a further benefit: for each meal purchased on the app, Feedback donates 10 per cent to Second Harvest, an organization that uses food that would otherwise be waste to prepare meals for the homeless. Ben Walters, Feedback's co-founder, admits that food insecurity wasn't a primary concern when developing the app, but once things got rolling, it only made sense to add a charitable element. They've got more planned, too: Walters hopes to pair businesses in the downtown core to charitable partners to whom leftovers from catered corporate lunches and banquets can be donated. 'For the first time ever, our generation really cares,' Walters suggests. Whether or not he's right, he's planning to capitalize on the idea that his target demographic has a conscience – and is that really so unconscionable, in the end?

Where Walters might have suggested he's part of the 'food industry,' he chose instead 'food space.' This makes sense: there's a division between what Walters does and what people who work in the food industry do, inasmuch as the latter physically interact with food. For Walters it's a space, to which he has applied design thinking: he identified a problem – waste at the consumer level, plus loss of profit – and solved for it. And he didn't lump anything else in.

Otherwise, he would have failed, or done two jobs only halfway. (Plus, Feedback's main consumer-facing element is cheap food; the user is essentially tricked into helping mitigate food waste *and* donating charitably.)

In *The Human Age*, Ackerman calls us 'masters of the invisible':

> We believe in television and radio waves, gnomelike quarks, GPS, microwaves, the World Wide Web, goslin photons, a mantilla of nerve endings in the brain, the voiceless hissing of background fizz from the big Bang, planets orbiting many stars in the night sky – some hospitable to life. Then there's all the panting eyes, throbbing jellies, iridescent bladders, and glowing mouths haunting the remote sunless abysses of the deep sea.

But, as far as food is concerned, we're blindly obsessed with the tangible – even Mark Zuckerberg, in his 2011 'annual challenge,' decided he wouldn't eat any meat that came from an animal he had not personally vanquished. But there is profound untapped power in applying our dependence on the convenience and instantaneous satisfaction of the invisible waves and wires and bits and bytes that connect us all to also feeding us all.

This, I believe, is where the personalized approach to food becomes so appealing for its potential potency; where the Food Computer and the food-waste-solving app step in; where the power in Musk's assertion that 'food is the new internet,' whatever he may have meant by it, might truly lie: if we put the future of food in smart-phone-owning people's pockets, right beside Uber and Foursquare, we might get somewhere.

But is this road – which at this point exists only, really, in theory – the one to take? If Silicon Valley gets involved, though – or *when* Silicon Valley gets involved – democratic, egalitarian, and moral principles will need to be involved from the planning stages. Tech giants have failed catastrophically on these fronts in the past: just look at Facebook, whose platform gave users the ability to influence the political process in ways that were, apparently, out of the hands of its founders and engineers.

Software engineers and social-media moguls have not planned their inventions to account for human opportunism (or maybe they did, but let's give them the benefit of the doubt at this time; maybe all Mark Zuckerberg has wanted, all along, is just to connect people, and nothing more). That's a hard thing to do. There's no real way to account, in the design of a tool, for how every single person in an audience of several billion will learn to manipulate it. Facebook learned the hard way. And if food is, indeed, the new internet, the ways in which information technology and software developers will begin to intersect with food systems and sustainability will, in theory, become widespread and readily accessible, at the same time fraught with opportunity for monetization, privatization, data manipulation, and exclusion. It's difficult to take at face value that all Kimbal Musk wants is #realfood for all – particularly considering the history of tech giants like Monsanto, whose capital-driven agricultural interventions essentially ruined the playing field for agribusiness, never mind decimating the livelihoods of hundreds of farmers in the process. This becomes more difficult when acknowledging that Musk's brother, Elon, and Zuckerberg are known for their egos – if food production ends up in the hands of megalomaniacal tech geniuses, things could get dystopian faster than they get sustainable.

And that's assuming things will get anywhere at any speed at all. Depending entirely on tech giants to solve for sustainability may be like depending on Tesla to sell us all electric cars – progress, on the somewhat disruptive front, moves slowly; it's more about peddling ideas and changing the ideological tide than putting actual, tangible things into people's hands. At least for now. It's the small-scale tech – the apps, the food computers – that might enact large-scale change. One thing the locavore lobby has gotten right is that sustainability truly does start at home; considering the issues plaguing our food growth and distribution chains, the whole thing isn't going to blow up at once.

And if we do put our future in the hands of the Musks et al., it might be prudent to take Facebook as a perfect example of how an incredible piece of technology can have its potential for good (or, at least, its potential for neutrality) manipulated beyond its intended use. If the morally agnostic-at-best social-media boom of the early 2000s is viewed as a road map of what *not* to do in the case of OpenAg and Kimbal Musk's incubators, things could turn out well.

Conclusion
You Say Tomato

You need an entire life just to know about tomatoes.
– Ferran Adrià

I grew up eating good tomatoes – good as in they tasted amazing, because they came from the backyard. Conversations about the issues plaguing our food systems often use the tomato as an illustrative example: Barry Estabrook wrote a whole book about it, *Tomatoland*, in 2011; *Food, Inc.* begins with Michael Pollan's assertion that the supermarket tomato is 'the idea of a tomato'; in Toronto, Mark Bittman was aghast to be accused of loving heirloom tomatoes above their more accessible supermarket cousins.

But the fact is that today's supermarket tomato is much less akin to the heirloom tomato – or the tomato of my youth. To paraphrase Pollan, it's more like the shadow of a tomato than like the flavourful fruit we all think we know. Partly this is to do with production, time of harvest, and the distance many tomatoes travel before they reach supermarket shelves. And it's because of the type of tomatoes farmers largely choose to grow: high-yield crops that produce more reliable outputs by volume, but less reliable products by nutritional density.

Recently, I've begun to wonder about whether the sad state of the average tomato has to do with the way the actual *planet* they're growing on is changing. In 2012, mathematician and biologist Irakli Loladze published a paper theorizing that, because of higher levels of atmospheric carbon dioxide, plants are growing bigger and faster –

which, on paper, would be a good thing, except that the speedier growth is giving plants less opportunity to develop nutrients, and the result is a less nutritious fruit. This is bad news for people who depend on plants to survive, but it's especially bad when you think back to *The Dorito Effect*: we're hardwired into knowing, evolutionarily and instinctively, that tastier food is more nutritionally dense, because it is. So could it be possible that Loladze's tomatoes, which are less nutritionally dense, are also Pollan's tomatoes, which are tasteless ideas of tomatoes? When we eat 'the idea of a tomato,' our brains say to us, *This tomato has nothing for you*. And most tomatoes are idea-tomatoes – except the heirloom stuff, which no one can afford, but since the heirloom stuff is growing on the same planet as the other stuff, it's probably losing a lot of its nutritional power, too.

The risk here is that, as plants drink up more CO_2 and grow less and less nutritionally dense, and therefore less delicious, people will gravitate toward packaged and processed foods that are engineered to taste good. And if we want to avoid this – if we're going to stick to the line of thinking that we ought to eat as little processed food as possible – we're going to have to start strategically processing the plants themselves.

In *The Dorito Effect*, Mark Schatzker tells the story of Harry Klee, a Florida-based tomato farmer who has spent years isolating and studying aromatic compounds in different breeds of tomatoes to determine which ones make tomatoes sweet, and by how much, and to whom, and to what degree. Klee has come up with a list of 'the 20 most important aromatic compounds in a tomato,' each of which 'is built from an essential nutrient.' His goal: to take tomatoes that have a high concentration of these flavour genes, breed them with one another, and reintroduce to the supermarket a tomato that tastes, yes, like a tomato your grandmother would recognize.

Despite Klee's work having something to do with genetics – and having the potential to allow farmers to test on a genetic level whether they have a good-tasting tomato varietal without actually tasting the tomato itself – and his past employment with Monsanto, he's not creating genetically modified tomatoes. Klee simply made an observation ('Some tomatoes taste sweeter'), asked some questions ('Are sweeter tomatoes more nutritious?'), formed a hypothesis ('Yes, they are'), developed a methodology of testing his hypothesis, and is working toward a conclusion. You might recognize this formula for the scientific method because you had it hammered into your head in elementary school, and you likely have seen for yourself that it works. Whether or not you end up proving or disproving what you set out to prove or disprove, you'll always, without fail, prove or disprove *something*. And information, especially as far as our volatile food systems are concerned, will always be more actionable than ideology.

On a similar wavelength, but doing markedly different work, is Joanne Chory. In 2017, Chory earned the Breakthrough Award in Life Sciences for her discovery that the addition of suberin – also known as cork – into plants that *aren't* cork allows them to intake and metabolize significantly higher levels of CO_2 than normal. What's more, suberin can last thousands of years, and Chory is experimenting with adding the compound into the roots of plants, specifically chickpeas; these roots can then, theoretically, store carbon dioxide underground for centuries.

Even better news: 'The numbers say you need about five percent of the world's farmland growing highly-enriched suberin crops to fix 50% of all the CO_2 that we're putting up there,' Chory told *Popular Mechanics*.

I don't know about you, but that data seems a lot more logical to me than trying to save the planet one feel-good ten-dollar bunch of organic radishes at a time. And that, perhaps, is the key: the slow-food movement and all its attendant food movements don't actually reverse any of humanity's gravest sins, when it comes to food. Instead, what they're there to do is right there in the name – slow things down, by making us feel bad about anything that speeds things up, or keeps pace.

Hopefully you have now developed a bit of an appetite for changing the way you think about sustainable food, if not the way you shop for and consume it. If so, there are steps you can take to help our collective approach to the future of food become a bit more egalitarian and innovative, and a little less fraught with guilt.

The first – and most significant – of these is to stop talking about 'good food' and 'bad food.' The words *good* and *bad* really don't work when it comes to calories we use to fuel our bodies. If food is unhealthy, call it unhealthy; if it's bad for the environment, call it bad for the environment; if it's genetically engineered, call it genetically engineered. Using the right language to discuss any given problem is key to understanding how to solve that problem – and using *good* and *bad* as indicators of the moral viability of food and food processes, frankly, hasn't gotten us anywhere. Push yourself to understand why certain foods are welcome in your pantry and others aren't. This may require reading beyond the headline, and dismantling existing biases concerning what makes food good vs. what makes food bad. Disinvesting the way we talk about food security and sustainability of their status symbolism and moral framing will help us to better understand what to do about it.

Once that's done, begin making the best possible decisions for *yourself* – whether that means buying organic only when you can afford it, consciously opting out of fast food even when you only have time to buy something pre-prepared, or simply forgiving yourself for occasionally making a purchase you know is not in the best interest of your body or your bank statement. It's more important to know why you're eating what you're eating than to blindly adhere to a unified culinary ideology all of the time.

A few months ago, in late spring, I went to visit my parents for a weekend, mainly to take a look at my mom's emerging vegetable garden. While we had dinner on my first night at home, she began excitedly telling me about a carton of eggs she'd seen at a downtown independent grocery story: each of the twelve eggs in the carton was a different colour and a different size than the egg before it – 'The way eggs are supposed to look,' she said. She was so thrilled by these eggs, but she couldn't bring herself to buy them; at about ten dollars for a mere dozen, the price was simply too high, no matter how virtuous (and beautiful) the product.

The next afternoon, we visited the same store, ostensibly to shop, but mostly to visit those eggs. They were just as she'd described: like a dozen pastel snowflakes, each a different shape, size, and colour than the one before it. Their cartons bore the name of their farmer, Murray Thunberg, an acquaintance of mine with a farm just outside Toronto. I've bought several Thanksgiving turkeys from

Murray's Farm and, once, a share of an entire butchered pig. Murray supplies his wares to restaurants as well as small, niche grocers; among his clientele is Langdon Hall, the restaurant and hotel whose dining room requires that men wear dinner jackets, and where Drake shot some of the promotional art for his 2016 album *Views*. It's expensive and exclusive, in other words – perfect for Murray's eggs. Which, by the way, I can confirm are absolutely delicious.

But on my income? They're not worth the price. Beside Murray's eggs at the grocery store in Guelph were cartons from Rowe Farms, a much larger and more widely distributed operation. They were priced at $5.99; these are the eggs I buy at home, in Toronto, and the ones my mother buys for her home, in Guelph. Both of us are armed with enough information to know that Murray's eggs come from happy, healthy chickens, and we therefore both have some feeling that the most morally correct decision is the more expensive of the two eggs. But purchasing that egg means we might have to compromise somewhere else, buying cheaper meat, imported tomatoes, a box of Kraft Dinner for supper one night later in the week. The $8.99 egg is perhaps a sustainable food, but for me and my mother, its purchase is not a sustainable habit.

And so we choose the middle ground, because there is absolutely a worse egg out there than the Rowe Farms egg. It is, in other words, the best possible decision for my mother to make, and for me to make, having considered all factors. By continuing to make the same decisions, as far as food is concerned, without any flexibility for new information, we would shoot ourselves in the foot; we'd end up with no money to buy anything but the cheapest egg of all. This is less a case of making decisions that are sustainable, because the second something is deemed sustainable, it stops *being* sustainable – every factor dictating sustainability, as far as food is concerned, is in constant motion; sticking to one idea has always put us at a disadvantage in this regard. It's better to eat responsibly, factoring in not only the world around us, but also our own individual worlds.

No problem has ever been solved by two polarized factions digging in their heels and hoping the other will concede. In food, as in life, middle ground is important: for as long as there are humans on earth, humans will need to eat; at the same time, for as long as humans will need to eat, we'll be responsible for every single process having to do with our food. I don't think we've figured out what the right process is, because we haven't figured out how to compromise (again: in food, as in life). We have all the tools, though. It's just a matter of sitting down at the same table and figuring out how to use them together.

Works Cited

Ackerman, Diane. *The Human Age*. Toronto: HarperCollins, 2014.

Armstrong, Karen. 'Metaphysical mistake.' *The Guardian*. (London) July 12, 2009.

Baggini, Julian. 'Clean eating and dirty morals: how food became a matter of morals.' *The Guardian*. (London.) July 17, 2016. Published online.

Barclay, Eliza. 'A Nation of Meat Eaters: See how it all adds up.' *The Salt*, National Public Radio. (New York City) June 27, 2012.

Bereznak, Alyssa. 'Buying the Farm.' *The Ringer*. April 11, 2017.

Bittemiller Evich, Helena. 'The great nutrient collapse.' *Politico*. (Arlington County) September 13, 2017.

Bittman, Mark. *A Bone to Pick*. New York City: Random House of Canada, 2015.

Bittman, Mark. 'Is "Eat Real Food" Unthinkable?' *The New York Times*. (New York City) February 8, 2011.

Bland, Alastair. 'Is the Livestock Industry Destroying the Planet?' *Smithsonian Magazine*. (Washington, D.C.) August 1, 2012.

Brilliat-Savarin, Jean Anthelme. *The Physiology of Taste*. Merchant Books, 2009.

Cho, Renee. 'How Green is Local Food?' *State of the Planet* (Earth Institute, Columbia University). (New York) September 4, 2012.

Childs, Natalie. 'The fruits of unpaid labour.' *Guts*. (Toronto) November 10, 2015.

Cox, Kate and Joe Fassier. 'It's the end of "organic" as we know it.' *The New Food Economy*. (New York City) November 2, 2017.

Desrocheres, Pierre, and Hiroko Shimizu. *The Locavore's Dilemma: In Praise of the 1,000-Mile Diet*. New York City: Public Affairs, 2012.

Dumych, Daniel M. *Images of America: Niagara Falls*. Chicago: Arcadia, 1996.

Eberhardt, Mark E. *Feeding the Fire*. New York City: Random House, 2007.

Ekers, Michael and Charles Levkoe. 'Ecological farm internships: Models, experiences and justice.' 2017. foodandlabour.ca

Estabrook, Barry. *Tomatoland*. Kansas City: Andrews McMeel. 2011.

Ferris, Jody L. 'Data Privacy and Regulation in the Agriculture Industry: Is it Necessary?' *Minnesota Journal of Law, Science and Technology*. 18.1 (2017).

Florida, Richard. *The New Urban Crisis*. New York City: Basic Books, 2017.

Folger, Tim. 'The Next Green Revolution.' *National Geographic Magazine*. (Washington, D.C.) September 2014.

Food Evolution. Dir. Scott Hamilton Kennedy. Black Valley Films, 2018. Digital stream.

Food Inc. Dir. Robert Kenner. Magnolia Pictures, 2009. Digital stream.

Food Statistics: 2009. Statistics Canada. Accessed online.

Frazier, Ian. 'The Vertical Farm.' *The New Yorker*. (New York City) January 9, 2017.

Fresco, Louis O. 'Splat goes the theory.' *Aeon*. (Melbourne) November 10, 2015.

Halwell, Brian. 'Why Kimbal Musk Is a Founding Father of the Modern Food Movement.' *Edible Manhattan*. (New York City) October 27, 2017.

Haspel, Tamar. 'Junk food is cheap and healthful food is expensive, but don't blame the farm bill.' *The Washington Post*. (Washington, D.C.) December 4, 2017.

Haspel, Tamar. 'Organic Food Fight!' *Slate*. (New York City) November 14, 2017.

Honore, Carl. *In Praise of Slow*. Toronto: Random House of Canada, 2004.

Hughes, Kathryn. 'Don't look down on those who eat fast food.' *The Guardian*. (London) June 8, 2014.

Jacobs, Jane. *The Death and Life of Great American Cities*. New York City: Vintage Books, 1961.

Jasper, Clint. 'United States farmers concerned about data privacy and precision agriculture technology.' *ABC News Australia*. (Sydney) September 2, 2014.

Kingsolver, Barbara. *Animal, Vegetable, Miracle*. New York City: HarperCollins, 2007.

Klein, Naomi. *No Logo*. Toronto: Random House, 2000

Madrigal, Alexis C. 'Chart: When will we eat hamburgers grown in test tubes?' *The Atlantic*. (Washington, D.C.) August 6, 2013.

Matthews, H. Scott and Christopher L. Weber. 'Food-miles and the relative climate impacts of food choices in the United States.' *Environmental Science & Technology*. 42.10 (2008).

McMahon, Tamsin. 'Is local food bad for the economy?' *Maclean's*. (Toronto) July 9, 2012.

Newitz, Annalee. 'Stop it with your anti-fast food moralizing.' *Gizmodo*. (New York City) June 10, 2014. Online.

Planet Earth II. Dir. Fredi Devas. BBC, 2016. DVD.

Pollan, Michael. *The Omnivore's Dilemma*. New York City: Penguin, 2006.

Reusing, Andrea. 'Farm-To-Table May Feel Virtuous, But It's Food Labor That's Ripe For Change.' *The Salt*, National Public Radio. (New York City) July 30, 2017.

Ross, Isabelle and Franzi Ross. 'My food struggle in pictures: When what I ate made me "good" or "bad".' National Public Radio. (New York City). May 7, 2017. Online.

Schatzker, Mark. *The Dorito Effect*. New York City: Simon & Schuster, 2015.

Sparapani, Tim. 'How Big Data And Tech Will Improve Agriculture, From Farm To Table.' *Forbes*. (New York City) March 23, 2017.

Steele, Dale, P.Ag. *Analysis of Precision Agriculture Adoption and Barriers in Western Canada*. April 2017. Prepared for Agriculture and Agri-Food Canada.

Thompson, Avery. 'The New Plants that Could Save Us from Climate Change.' *Popular Mechanics*. (New York City) December 3, 2017.

Tweedie, Neil. 'Jamie Oliver's ministry of marvels.' *The Daily Telegraph*. (London) November 6, 2009.

'U of G Professor wins innovation award for HIR technology.' *Canadian Poultry*. May 9, 2017.

Viviano, Frank. 'This Tiny Country Feeds the World.' *National Geographic Magazine*. (Washington, D.C.) September 2017.

Weiler, Anelyse. 'Migrant farm workers and Ontario's food movement: Finding common cause.' *Sustainontario.com*. March 24, 2015.

Wilson, Amanda. 'The new Canadian agricultural partnership: Dancing to the same old tune?' *Foodsecurecanada.org*.

Acknowledgements

Many, many thanks to Emily Keeler, without whose faith, insight, and immense patience this book never would have happened, as well as to Alana Wilcox, Jessica Rattray, and the rest of the remarkable Coach House family. To Evan Fraser, Kelly Hodgins, Will Bergmann, Hannah Hunter, Kevin Folta, and everyone else who spoke to me about the incredible, innovative stuff they're doing on their farms and in their labs, and the innumerable hundreds – Arlene Stein at Terroir, Val Howes in print and in person, Murray Thunberg on his farm in Cambridge, Nick Saul at Community Food Centres Canada, Josh Hume over dinner, and Joshna Maharaj at…well, everywhere – whose work in and around food has inspired, informed, and galvanized my own curiosity over the years. To my friends, for putting up with my shit and providing endless support and encouragement while I got this done – thank you to Tanner Cormier, Hailey McCron, Alysha Whyte-Guerriero, Ilana Korn and, especially and extraordinarily, to Mark Wheler. And finally, to my family: to my sister, Emily, for consistently being my other half for lack of a better term; to my father, Darrell, for teaching me humor and resilience, and to my mother, Lelia, for showing me how good a person can be. I love you all.

Rebecca Tucker is a Toronto-based writer, editor, and journalist, whose work has covered food, travel, arts, and culture. Her writing has appeared in the *National Post* and *Globe and Mail*, as well as *Vice*, *Buzzfeed*, *Reader's Digest* magazine, and *Toronto Life*. She holds a bachelor's degree in journalism from Ryerson University, and lives in Toronto's west end with her cat, Sam.

About the
Exploded Views Series

Exploded Views is a series of probing, provocative essays that offer surprising perspectives on the most intriguing cultural issues and figures of our day. Longer than a typical magazine article but shorter than a full-length book, these are punchy salvos written by some of North America's most lyrical journalists and critics. Spanning a variety of forms and genres – history, biography, polemic, commentary – and published simultaneously in all digital formats and handsome, collectible print editions, this is literary reportage that at once investigates, illuminates, and intervenes.

www.chbooks.com/explodedviews

Typeset in Goodchild Pro and Gibson Pro. Goodchild was designed by Nick Shinn in 2002 at his ShinnType foundry in Orangeville, Ontario. Shinn's design takes its inspiration from French printer Nicholas Jenson who, at the height of the Renaissance in Venice, used the basic Carolingian minuscule calligraphic hand and classic roman inscriptional capitals to arrive at a typeface that produced a clear and even texture that most literate Europeans could read. Shinn's design captures the calligraphic feel of Jensen's early types in a more refined digital format. Gibson was designed by Rod McDonald in honour of John Gibson FGDC (1928–2011), Rod's long-time friend and one of the founders of the Society of Graphic Designers of Canada. It was McDonald's intention to design a solid, contemporary, and affordable sans serif face.

Printed at the old Coach House on bpNichol Lane in Toronto, Ontario, on Rolland Opaque Natural paper, which was manufactured, acid-free, in Saint-Jérôme, Quebec, from 50 per cent recycled paper, and it was printed with vegetable-based ink on a 1972 Heidelberg KORD offset litho press. Its pages were folded on a Baumfolder, gathered by hand, bound on a Sulby Auto-Minabinda, and trimmed on a Polar single-knife cutter.

Series editor: Emily M. Keeler
Cover illustration by Chloe Cushman
Author photo by Paul Terefenko

Coach House Books
80 bpNichol Lane
Toronto ON M5S 3J4
Canada

416 979 2217
800 367 6360

mail@chbooks.com
www.chbooks.com